SAVING SHANNON

SAVING SHANNON

A Family's Story of Strength and Devotion

PAUL J. MULHERN

ISBN: 979-8-9856193-0-0

All the names of those not in my immediate family have been changed to protect each person's privacy. Conversations that occurred have been re-created based on notes I recorded. They are not verbatim of the discussion but do represent the general tenor of the conversation.

Dedicated to all my brothers and sisters,
whose support and consistent input helped us
emerge from the darkness and find our way back to health.

TABLE OF CONTENTS

PROLOGUE

I tossed all my gear into the car and departed Fort Drum, New York, after completing two weeks of US Army Reserve annual training. As a captain, I had an advisory role with a military police company. My unit was based in Willow Grove, Pennsylvania, about an hour from my residence in Sewell, New Jersey. We supported units based at Fort Drum by providing military police, medics, and personnel specialists. I was glad to share my knowledge in firearms and defensive tactics with young soldiers. Most of it I'd acquired in my full-time job with the US Customs Service. I noticed some dents in my car door, which had to have occurred during an exercise in which I'd been a noncompliant role player and had to be forcibly taken down. What were a few dents and a few bruises? I had completed the training and earned the extra money to support my family. I enjoyed most of these activities but not the exercises that included canine teams that took me down. The dogs did not seem to know it was a training exercise. Fortunately, an arm sleeve prevented their teeth from penetrating my skin.

The late May weather was beautiful at seventy degrees and sunny. The highway was free of traffic and surrounded by beautiful rolling hills on both sides. They reminded me of the mountains in Bavaria, Germany, which I got to know well from the turret of an M1A1 Abrams tank. My active-duty time prepared me for this reserve gig. We spent most of that year in Bavaria in the field on training exercises or patrolling the Inner German border.

At this rate I would be home in four hours to see my girls. I missed my wife, Jan, and my daughter, Shannon. Jan's sister Tara was visiting from overseas. That gave me lots of time with Shannon as the girls caught up. Jan and I had met at JFK Airport, where I worked for US Customs and she worked for an airline. We dated for over a year and overcame the challenge of different cultures and multiple attempts by jealous coworkers to break us up. I transferred to the Port of Philadelphia, and we eagerly got married and started a family. Shannon was our bundle of joy whose personality kept us laughing. All appeared headed in the right direction as we had a nice suburban home, secure careers, and a daughter who stole our hearts every day.

I pulled into a truck stop for gas and snacks—truck stops have the best food and an assortment of small entertaining toys, and the truckers' personalities are always on display. Shannon and I enjoyed talking to truckers in rest stops and asking what they were carrying that day. We both laughed at the truckers' shuffles from so much sitting at the wheel. At three years of age, Shannon had developed an imitation of tired truckers taking baby steps and moving slowly. She was happy to share this with anyone watching as I laughed my head off.

I arrived home on schedule, and the girls were happy to see me. Shannon grabbed my arm and pulled me to her playroom, where she was watching new highlights of *Tom and Jerry* cartoons. She showed me a segment of Tom being offered a million dollars to stop abusing Jerry. He could not resist the temptation and continued to smack Jerry and commented that "he had lost a million dollars but was happy." Shannon found that part hilarious and played it several times. She was moving away from her Barney the Dinosaur tapes and getting more interested in the Disney classics. She proudly showed me her new copy of *Tarzan*, which had been in the theaters only one year ago, and displayed her new skill of popping out the *Cinderella* video tape and inserting *Tarzan*, hitting play, and turning up the volume.

1

DECELEBRATING JULY FOURTH

It was a spectacular July morning, with the temperature reaching eighty, no humidity, and bright sunny skies, and I was working US Customs operations at the Philadelphia airport. We checked several flights departing the country to Caribbean destinations for passengers with undeclared currency. If someone was evading currency-reporting requirements, it usually meant the cash was being exported in return for some inbound illegal importations. There were several high-risk passengers who had just short of the undeclared $10,000 mark we were seeking for penalty action. Next, we examined cargo inbound from African or European countries for narcotic concealments and did a thorough job despite the frustration of rarely finding contraband. We stumbled upon a barrel of personal effects destined for Jamaica. Document review determined it was being exported by the same passenger we had checked that morning who was very nervous. X-ray images revealed soap, toys, and food products on the screen. All were popular products shipped out frequently to Caribbean countries. A manual exam was also negative. We were accustomed to negative exam results despite high-risk indicators based on a shipment's origin or destination. But nothing could reduce my enthusiasm for being off the next two days to celebrate July Fourth with my daughter and wife concurrent with my birthday.

My three-year-old daughter had just started a summer preschool program. I took her on the first day, and she would not let go of me. Other parents quickly dropped their children and left. I tried to leave, but Shannon said, "Daddy, don't do this to me." The main teacher suggested I just leave, so I complied, hoping the crying Shannon would adjust. Day two was a little easier, and day three was great as Shannon grew comfortable with her new friends and arts and crafts activities.

Shannon had beautiful, long, dark-brown hair with natural curls and remarkably striking facial features—bright hazel eyes and a smile surrounded by the cutest dimples. Her beauty forced strangers to comment from a distance. Shannon always made people's day with her warm personality. She seemed to know people derived happiness from talking to her. She loved the attention. On a day trip to Ocean City, New Jersey, she celebrated arriving at the boardwalk by spinning around and laughing at the seagulls. A group of older women on a nearby bench started rejoicing in her enthusiasm. Shannon recognized this and started to run after the seagulls as the women laughed at such spirit. Some referred to her as a young Shirley Temple or made comparisons to the gorgeous girl dancing in a Pepsi commercial. Shannon had taken all of the good features from her Mom's Eastern European descent and my Irish lineage and combined them to create a stunning profile.

Furthermore, Shannon's personality was unstoppable. She loved to act silly and was hooked on PBS shows and Disney movies. She seemed to have superhuman strength, needing only six hours of sleep a night and a two-hour nap in the afternoon. Shannon displayed the style and maturity of someone much older.

"India 1036, this is India 1000."

The US Customs radio interrupted my summer thoughts as I wondered why someone would be calling me so close to the end of my shift. Probably some correction of a monthly report from June was required. We were wrapping up cargo exams, hoping to discover contraband for our enforcement action, to no avail.

"India 1000, this is India 1036," I answered as I have done hundreds of times.

"India 1036, 10-21 India 1001 at the International Arrivals Building?"

"India 1036, roger," I responded, hoping I could push any new admin task to when I returned on Thursday. India 1001 was the chief inspector; what could he possibly want?

I drove back to the US Customs Cargo office to close out the shift, hoping Shannon had had a good day in preschool. As I pulled into the parking lot, the radio blared out again, requesting I call the chief inspector right away. This had to be something more important than monthly stats. What else could be going on? I went to the office to make the call and was stopped by a supervisor from the Cargo Clearance section, who had a look of utter fear on her face, sort of like she felt a deep sense of empathy for me.

"Paul, the chief inspector just called and said your daughter has been airlifted to Cooper Trauma Center."

These words no parent ever plans for sent chills up my spine and hit me with waves of shock.

"What happened to her?"

"I really don't know; does she go to school?"

"Yes."

"Maybe she was injured at school."

"Which Cooper—the trauma center in Camden? There are lots of hospitals that are part of the Cooper network."

"I guess the one in Camden."

"Should I take Ben Franklin Bridge or Walt Whitman?"

"I don't know; are you OK to drive? Let me call the chief and try to get more information. Should I give you a ride?"

"I can drive myself—my daughter is so active. I'm sure she will be all right."

I grabbed my gear and ran to my car, a one-year-old Hyundai Elantra. I noticed my body shaking as I hit the stairs. My breathing was accelerated as fear spread throughout my body in seconds.

Stay calm, I kept telling myself. *She will be all right. Put everything in God's hands. Focus on your breathing and drive safely. Make a point to reassure Jan, who is on scene and has to be hysterical.*

Shannon was a remarkably healthy child. She had only had one ear infection in three years and a couple of viruses. She was strictly a breastfed baby. Jan never handled Shannon's minor illnesses well, so distressed to see her only child suffering in any way.

The traffic was not bad for a sunny July day just before a major holiday. I drove carefully, but compliance with the traffic laws was the furthest thing from my mind. Shannon did have a habit of recklessly jumping and playing without taking some important precautions, as most kids her age did.

Had she fallen and broken a leg or arm? Hopefully it was no more serious than that. Why had they airlifted her to the trauma center? Perhaps a helicopter ambulance crew was responding to any case to increase flight training time?

Deep down, I knew I was denying the facts. Helicopters are only brought when necessary, and Cooper Trauma Center was renowned. People often joked that Cooper had so much experience from treating urban violence victims from the surrounding slums. My daughter could be in a life-and-death struggle, I thought, and I had to be with her.

I considered a couple of routes and decided on Interstate 95 North to the Walt Whitman Bridge, then onto River Road, through the heart of Camden to the hospital. I had recently worked on a Seaport Enforcement Team that covered neighboring piers, and I knew this area like the back of my hand. I could avoid Jersey Shore traffic and minimize the chance of getting stopped for speeding. I actually had taken a colleague to the Cooper ER to get a sliced finger sewn up. Camden was an economically depressed city of ninety thousand residents. The vast majority of residents were minorities. The residents suffered from high unemployment rates and poverty. Millions of federal dollars had gone to Camden in the past decade to create a waterfront full of tourist attractions. The redevelopment funds did not go very far as the city was full of blighted houses and teenage parents.

The closer I got to the hospital, the faster my heart beat. I just hoped for the best and focused on the confidence in my daughter's determination and the power of prayer. I finally saw the red signs for the ER and made a few abrupt turns before carelessly creating my own parking place in the crowded lot. I burst into the hospital and immediately set off the metal detector with my service weapon and the full uniform still on. An overweight security guard told me weapons were not permitted in the ER. I produced my US Customs credentials and explained my daughter had just been flown in. She directed me to the waiting room, where I heard a very familiar crying sound before entering. Jan looked beyond devastated. She threw her arms around me.

"How is Shannon?"

"She was hit by a car and has a head injury."

"Is she OK?"

"No."

"What happened?"

"We were picking flowers in front of Green Tree Produce, and Shannon had a couple in her hand. The wind blew them away. She ran after them. A sport utility vehicle ran her over. We had just come from McDonald's, where Shannon climbed to the top of the outside playground."

I had questions about what they were doing there and how Shannon had gotten near the street but decided to focus on Shannon's condition and treatment. Jan was sobbing and breathing heavily while speaking. She was holding Shannon's white sandals and some type of small arts and crafts item and her cell phone. I reached out and held her trembling body.

"She made this little house at school today and was so proud of herself. She was dying to show you. Then we took Tara to work at Green Tree Produce and spent some time playing miniature golf since you weren't coming home until two thirty."

Jan was a tall blonde with long hair, a gorgeous face, and a firm figure. Her eyes were bloodshot from tears and her face red as a beet from shock. She was overcome with emotion and fear, but still had the presence of mind to call Shannon's pediatrician and suggest Shannon be transferred to Children's Hospital of Philadelphia, which was world renowned for treating children for complex illnesses and injuries. The local police drove Jan and her sister to the hospital in Camden. Shannon was transported to Cooper in a helicopter, which had landed in a school baseball field right next to the site of the accident. Township police also notified my agency to get me to the hospital as soon as possible.

Reception was weak in the ER waiting room, so I went to the parking lot and advised the pediatrician of the situation. He assured me that Cooper Trauma Center was the best place for my daughter right now. He said he would check on her in the following days. I paced up and down the walkway to the ER while I made this call. Panic was starting to set in.

I was devastated by the situation and knew I had to get control fast. I had a critically injured daughter, a hysterical wife, an equally panic-stricken sister-in-law, and I felt the effects of shock hitting my system instantly. My chest felt crushed. My stomach was doing somersaults. My head felt indescribably nauseating sensations. I decided to call in some backup.

The first call was to my sister Betty. I knew she was home because her husband was home recovering from a heart procedure. I briefed her in ten seconds and asked her to call my brother Barry, who is a lawyer specializing in medical malpractice, and asked her to notify my dad. They could focus on details I was too shocked to notice, notify the insurance company, and take charge. My dad had raised ten kids, sending them all to college. Both

Betty and Barry never took their noses off the grindstone and would know what to do. I needed some peer support too. The next call went to the Customs Operations desk. I reported my three year-old daughter was in a life-or-death situation and I needed two close friends named Kowoski and Surfer at the hospital. The duty officer responded they would be there in minutes. They were both family men and guys you felt you could take on an army with and be victorious.

Back in the ER waiting room, a guard saw me still in uniform and jokingly asked me if I was there to relieve her. I saw my sister-in-law Tara in a corner section of the waiting room; she was more hysterical than my wife and was praying out loud for Shannon. She was staying with us for a few months and worked in the deli / ice cream / miniature golf joint where Shannon had been run over. My thoughts drifted to the establishment, which was on a busy street and had a large parking lot. Cars constantly arrived and departed, making it a dangerous place for kids. I was always aware of the danger and stressed being careful there when Jan dropped off Tara. Shannon had moved through the parking lot without incident but had been struck a few yards away. Feelings of rage surfaced, which I suppressed. I had to focus on the positive in order to get through this shocking event. Anger is not a productive emotion, so I chose to ignore it.

A woman in a nursing outfit came out of the ER to talk to us.

"Your daughter's vital signs are stable. She is breathing with the help of a ventilator. We are taking her for a CAT scan now and will know more after that."

"Is she moving?"

"The type of movement we see tells us she has a brain injury. She is posturing, which means turning her arms and legs inward."

"Can we see her?"

"Yes. She will be coming out of these doors soon to go for the CAT scan."

I knew nothing about brain injuries other than that they were serious and thought any movement was a good sign. Tara said she could not see

Shannon and would stay in the waiting room to continue praying.

Jan continued to cry and had gone through at least a hundred tissues. She clung to Shannon's shoes as if there was no tomorrow. I did not want Shannon to see her like this.

"We are going to see Shannon and talk to her and reassure her that she will be all right," I told the two of them. "Her vitals are stable, and she is a tough kid. She will be OK. You will be strong for Shannon."

Several nurses barged through the doors with Shannon, asleep on a mobile hospital bed. She had a cervical collar around her neck that appeared to be very uncomfortable. Bruises ran across her forehead and face, and there was a deep cut above her lip. Both of her shoulders were badly bruised. She looked battered, but somehow her spirit of life was present and visible. At least two IVs were connected to her arms. A breathing tube ran down her throat, attached to a ventilator apparatus. She was unconscious, oblivious to everything around her, I thought. Nausea overwhelmed me, and cold chills ran up my spine. I tried to ignore these foreign feelings and summoned the strength to talk to her.

"Shannon, everything will be OK. I'm done with work today and off for the next two days. Mom said you had fun at school. Great job on the house you made and on climbing to the top of the playground at McDonald's. The doctors and nurses will take care of you, and you will be all right."

Jan steadfastly stood by me even though she lost the struggle with her tears. She told Shannon over and over, "I love you, honey."

They wheeled our daughter away and told us they would take her to the third-floor pediatric intensive care unit (PICU) after the CAT scan was finished and the doctor would talk to us then. Jan, Tara, and I started upstairs. I supported one in each arm and felt the dead weight as we walked to the elevator. I tried to reassure them that Shannon would be all right. They had seen the SUV strike her and had a much tougher time being optimistic.

We rode the elevator to the third floor and sat down in another waiting area. My own feelings of fear began to resist the forces of optimism. I tried to stay positive as the hospital chaplain arrived on the scene. I gave him a quick overview of my daughter's critical situation as Jan and Tara sobbed uncontrollably.

The chaplain wore a white collar, but I was not sure of his denomination. He assured us that all young children belong to God and their ascension to heaven is certain. He said a nice prayer asking God to protect our daughter. The three of us felt a little better after hearing the chaplain's words.

Jim Kowoski and Tom "Surfer" Wolf from US Customs arrived just as the chaplain was leaving. They both were wearing field uniforms and had worked up quite a sweat examining sea cargo for contraband before rushing down here. Shipments that arrived via the seaport were bigger and more strenuous to inspect. They had clearly dropped what they were doing and answered the call; I was incredibly relieved at their arrival.

"Hey, Tom and Jim. Thanks for coming out. Shannon was struck by an SUV and has a head injury. They brought her here on a helicopter, and she is getting a CAT scan now. We saw her, and she is on a ventilator and has lots of bumps and bruises but does not look bad. Right now I am just focusing on the positive signs."

"That's all you can do, Paul."

I suddenly burst into tears and buried my face and arms into the back of a chair. I had been hiding my emotions to be strong for the ladies, and they all came out at once. Tom and Jim rubbed my shoulders, encouraging me to let it out.

"Paul, her vital signs are stable, and she is in a great hospital, and she is a tough kid." Surfer spoke like a reassuring brother. "Remember, you trained her. She will be OK. Kowoski and I will get the entire Customs community praying and doing everything you need. Our families and parishes will say prayers for her. Your family and Jan's will do even more. Think of all the friends you have."

"You're right, Jim—Shannon is a ball of fire."

I stood up, having found the second wind I needed. My older brother

Barry arrived on the scene. He could think of administrative issues that needed attention. He had been working across the river about fifteen blocks into Philadelphia. Most of the lawyers had taken the day before the holiday off, but he'd been in the office. I advised him of the situation.

One of the ER nurses approached us and said our daughter was set up in the PICU and that Dr. O'Conner would speak to us regarding the CAT scan. She led us to a small meeting room with a table and four chairs. Jan and Tara sat down with the ER nurse, and Dr. O'Conner took his seat across the table. I remained standing with Barry, hoping for but not expecting good news. Dr. O'Conner was around fifty years of age with white hair and a white mustache, of medium height and build, and probably a smoker due to his husky voice. He gave the impression of being a veteran of ER trauma work and accustomed to briefing parents.

Surprisingly the ER nurse spoke first. She must have had an additional specialty in dealing with shocked families.

"Your daughter has two fractures in her skull that we are not worried about. They will heal. She has a small blood clot in her brain that we are not worried about. That will be absorbed into the bloodstream. She has swelling in the brain, which is the real problem."

Dr. O'Conner finally spoke. "We have to wait to see if the swelling in her brain increases overnight. I ordered a neurological consult, and they may want to insert a monitor into Shannon's skull to monitor intracranial pressure. The first forty-eight hours are the most critical. If the swelling does not increase, that is a good sign. Right now Shannon is unresponsive. She is in a coma. We have to wait for her to wake up. It may be days. It may be weeks. It may be months."

"What are her chances?" Jan asked.

"It is against policy to use percentages."

Waves of nausea rushed through my body, starting in my head, running past my stomach, and stopping at my knees, like someone had just whacked me with a baseball bat. Somehow I did not collapse. I had known this was a critical situation but had not been aware my daughter was fighting for her life.

Dr. O'Conner continued, "Shannon also has a small amount of fluid in her stomach. I'm not sure where it is from. We will watch that too. Let's hope Shannon has a good night, and we will know more in the morning."

The ER nurse closed out the meeting by saying, "Shannon is all set in the PICU now. I will take you to see her."

We walked back toward the PICU. As we passed the elevator doors, my dad and sister popped out. What a job Betty had done. She had gotten Dad, Barry, and herself here and found someone to watch her kids while her husband was home recovering from the previous day's procedure to stabilize his heart.

My dad must have been home working from his office. He formed his own insurance adjuster business upon turning seventy-five and had a legal photography business as well. He was one of those guys who relaxed by working. He was a proud grandfather of eighteen, and I knew he was using his close relationship with God to pray for Shannon's health. Barry briefed Dad and Betty on the medical situation as Jan and I were eager to see Shannon and provide whatever comfort we could. Tara still could not see Shannon and chose to stay in the conference room.

Our second visit in the hospital to see Shannon turned out to be more painful than the first. She was lying in bed with the top portion of her body elevated to enhance her breathing. She was hooked up to a ventilator with the breathing tube down her throat and had various connections displaying all sorts of numbers. Several IV lines were running to each of her arms, and the nurse was taping down an additional line to Shannon's forearm that seemed to be connected to a TV monitor. That monitor had constant readings of Shannon's blood pressure and heart rate. A catheter was connected to her bladder. The bruises to her face, forehead, and shoulders were more visible. The laceration on her upper lip looked like it was a half inch wide. Shannon must have turned over and over, repeatedly smacking the ground.

Shannon was rotating her arms and legs inward and arching her back like a drawbridge. This was a continuation of the posturing the ER nurse mentioned, a very bad sign. Posturing is a form of primitive movement. Shannon's brain could not communicate with her spinal cord, and the response was the involuntary movement of twisting her limbs inward. I told Shannon that her mom and dad were with her and would stay until she was all better. Jan kept stroking Shannon's hair and reassuring her in a soothing voice. She had stopped crying for the moment. Dad, Barry, Betty, Tom, and Jim were in the background and feeling as shocked as we were.

The PICU had four beds; only one other bed was occupied, by a four-year-old child suffering from a neurological problem that caused seizures. Curtains separated the beds, which provided little privacy. The nurse's station was only a few feet away, and it was very organized with computers and charts.

Dr. Saad Murza was standing next to Shannon's bed. He was wearing a surgical gown and had just inserted an arterial line for Shannon. Dr. Murza was of Pakistani descent, with dark skin and black hair; he weighed about 140 pounds and had a wiry frame, maybe five feet, seven inches tall. He was well groomed and very enthusiastic. He was the PICU attending physician, meaning he was the supervisor of the residents and in charge of this department.

Dr. Murza recognized us as Shannon's parents without an introduction and started his briefing. "Shannon is agitated right now. I will give her a dose of Versed to calm her down. We don't want her to yank out the IVs or the arterial line. We inserted a catheter in her bladder so she can urinate and an arterial line in her arm to draw blood. Her vitals are being constantly monitored, as you can see on the screen. Don't worry if you hear frequent beeps. It just means her blood pressure or pulse ox has jumped due to all of her movement."

I thought this was too much information too fast but was glad Dr. Murza was establishing himself as a subject matter expert.

Dr. Murza was a fast talker and drew few breaths. "I just saw her CAT scan and am encouraged by it because there is only a very small hemorrhage. The hemorrhage should be absorbed into the blood, and the fractures will heal in time. The real issue right now is how much additional swelling in her brain we will see. I am also encouraged by some of her movements. It is not all posturing. She has withdrawal from a painful stimulus and demonstrates brisk pupil response to a light stimulus. She has a fever right now, which is very common with brain injuries. We will give her Tylenol for that. Let's hope there is no additional swelling and she wakes up soon. Then we can consider removing the breathing tube."

Just as things could not have looked bleaker, we heard hopeful news from Dr. Murza. This guy was great. He explained things in layman's terms and was optimistic about Shannon, not necessarily in what he said but rather how he delivered it.

"I am waiting for consults from neurosurgery, the plastic surgeon for the laceration on her lip, as well as the rehab staff. The CAT scan also showed a small amount of fluid in her stomach. I am going to insert a tube that will extract that fluid. Please step out, and I will come get you when I am done."

We walked back to the meeting room and collapsed into the chairs. We briefed Tara on the good news. My dad, who had worked in the auto claims business for forty years, said he knew of cases where kids recovered from accidents like this in weeks. I turned my weapon over to Surfer for security as I would not be leaving the hospital any time soon. I gave my car keys to Kowoski so that he could move my car to the garage. Barry said he would notify the auto and health insurance companies and get a copy of the police report and start preliminary work on the case. Betty volunteered to notify the rest of the family, including six sisters and one brother, and get my sister Anne to visit tonight since she was a veteran physical therapist (PT) very familiar with the brain injury recovery process. Another chaplain visited us and said he was praying for Shannon. Kowoski and Surfer briefed him on the situation, and I overheard Kowoski say, "This guy is a great father. His daughter is his life."

The latter was certainly true as I was frustrated with career progression and Jan and I were dealing with the ups and downs that all couples experience. Shannon made me forget all the aggravation. Regarding my parenting skills, they were being tested in a tortuous way.

Gradually our guests left with promises to visit tomorrow. We returned to Shannon's bedside and comforted her the best we could. Tara had taken charge of notifying Jan's family of Shannon's condition. Jan was on her third box of tissues. I kept repeating that Shannon's remarkable energy and enthusiasm would pull her through this. Jan's mother had died of a heart attack in her early sixties ten months earlier. Jan was still grieving. I told my devastated wife that her mom had left early so she could be in a position to watch over Shannon and guide her through this unexpected trauma.

Shannon kept the PICU nurses busy as they frequently drew blood for lab samples, injected medicine into her IVs, and adjusted her position using pillows and sheets to keep her comfortable. I gave Shannon a two-hour speech telling her how proud I was of her school performance that day and that we would celebrate the Fourth of July and my birthday when she got out of the hospital very soon. I was confident that she could hear me. My monologue and Jan's participation with the nurses in caring for Shannon helped us burn some nervous energy.

My sister Anne, the PT, arrived just as the on-call neurosurgeon was checking Shannon. Anne was always on the go with a full-time job and three active boys. She was four years older than me and had lots of experience with patients with neurological conditions. We barely got to talk before the neurosurgeon had the results of his exam and CAT scan review. The neurosurgeon was a stocky, intense guy, about forty years old.

"The good news is I don't see significant amounts of swelling and bleeding on the CAT scan. There is a tiny amount of hemorrhaging in one area. There is no need to insert the intracranial monitor in her skull to measure pressure. We will hope the swelling and bleeding do not increase and she wakes up in the next seventy-two hours."

Anne and the doctor had a five-minute conversation in medical terms, mainly about shearing injuries that would not be visible on the CAT scan. The doctor finally said to us, "It is possible she experienced a shearing injury. That is a twisting or turning on the neurons and axons in the brain, and the recovery process is very long in those cases. We will do another CAT scan tomorrow and go from there."

Anne recognized Sharon's posturing limbs and immediately went to work ranging my daughter's feet and legs. She bent her feet back to their natural position and held them for fifteen seconds. Here was another thing we could do to help. Anne explained that Shannon's brain injury was affecting her body by increasing the spasticity of her muscles. Anne stretched and rotated Shannon to maintain blood flow and loosen up her stiff muscles. Anne continued to explain that the therapists would make hand and foot braces to maintain proper alignment and prevent deformities.

The phone started ringing with concerned coworkers and worried neighbors. I advised them that Shannon was in critical condition with a head injury and requested prayers for her to improve. My oldest sister, May Ellen, arrived. My wife's brothers arrived after making a two-hour trip from North Jersey. All had questions about Shannon's condition and prognosis, but we didn't have any answers. All we could do was hope and pray. The hospital was doing a great job, and my family was rising to the occasion. A PICU nurse arrived with a bag of blood saying that Shannon's blood was not clotting fast enough and she needed a blood transfusion. I was going to need both groups, family and medical, to do an amazing job to get through this.

Shannon's temperature started to rise and peaked at 104 degrees at 8:00 p.m. Nurses applied an air-conditioned blanket and cold towels to her head. These measures reduced her temperature to 100 by 10:00 p.m. Her blood pressure remained steady at 115 over 60. Her heart rate peaked at 180 and came down to the 140 range. Her respiration rate hovered at

20. Regular doses of Tylenol and Versed were working. I had never heard of Versed before but quickly learned it was to help her stay calm and not be so agitated by the breathing tube.

A young doctor and nurse appeared and introduced themselves as plastic surgery specialists there to sew up Shannon's lip. I went back to the waiting area and briefed the brothers-in-law on the numerous improvements. The plastic surgeon reappeared minutes later stating he was done and would take the stitches out in one week. I quietly hoped Shannon would be awake in one week. Removing sutures was the least of my problems.

Shannon with both Jan and me on her third birthday

2

SURVIVING THE MIDNIGHT RIDE

I sent Tara and the brothers-in-law back to our house for the night. Jan did quite a bit of praying while I resumed my monologue with my unresponsive daughter, which continued way past midnight. I reassured Shannon she would be all right. I went into detail about all the summer activities we would enjoy, such as the playground and trips to the beach and swimming pool. I told her stories from her favorite books from memory and made a note to bring the books from the house.

The respiration therapist stopped by every hour to suction Shannon's mucus by pulling the device up through the breathing tube since she could not cough it up on her own. He checked the settings on the machine and logged them in. They had to maximize the oxygen to Shannon's brain to reduce swelling. The brain has no room to expand when it swells because it is housed inside the skull. Swelling increases the pressure inside the brain due to the increased blood flow to swollen areas.

Shannon kept the nurse busy all night checking her IV lines, drawing blood, answering our constant questions, and adjusting her position in bed. Various doctors stopped by and checked Shannon mostly by reviewing her chart and talking to the nurse.

I continued to dig for positives.

- Shannon had been struck at 12:30 p.m. Local nurses were beside her in seconds, having stopped on their way to work.
- Paramedics were present in minutes.
- The air ambulance intubated Shannon to maximize airflow to her brain and transported Shannon to the trauma center fifteen minutes after she was struck.
- In the ER, doctors gave Shannon steroid-type medication to prevent seizures and lessen the brain swelling.
- Surgery was not required at this point.
- Remarkably Shannon had no broken bones.
- Shannon had survived the first night.
- Shannon's vital signs had remained stable.

The hour that immediately follows the point of injury is known as the "golden hour" in the medical community. It is the most important time for patients with brain injuries. Shannon had been given all the right treatment, and the neurosurgeon had determined an intracranial monitor was not necessary. He was also upbeat after seeing the CAT scan. The attending physician in the PICU also was optimistic. Family and friends were rallying around us. Maybe this would be an ordeal of days instead of months.

Morning came, and Jan and I were still running on adrenaline. A new nurse received a long briefing from the midnight-shift nurse. Lots of doctors checked in. Dr. O'Conner was clearly the most relieved that no emergency CAT scans had been required overnight and that Shannon's condition had not deteriorated. He said he would not examine Shannon, as the trauma doctor would. I guessed he was strictly assigned ER patients.

The previous day's ER nurse stopped by, and I bragged about Shannon's fever being down. She responded that we should expect it to return and fluctuate up and down. PTs and OTs (occupational therapists) stopped by and together checked every joint in Shannon's body by moving her limbs extensively. They seemed to be testing her reflexes and measuring what resistance she could provide. No healthy child could stand such an evaluation. Shannon was totally unaware that her limbs were being pulled and prodded in every direction. The therapists elaborated on what we already knew about posturing and started doing the same ranging exercises my sister Anne had done the night before. They saw the Beanie Baby dolls (a cat and a rabbit) we had put in her hands and said it was a good idea to have placed them there. The PT said "space boots" would be made to keep Shannon's feet straight. She explained they were specially designed orthopedic footwear that would keep Shannon's feet straight and could be adjusted as the condition improved. The OT said she would make special braces for Shannon's hands. Anne's suggestions had been right on target. We were glad for all the treatment but devastated at Shannon being unresponsive despite being stretched like a ballet dancer.

We finally got a break as the therapists left, and we took a seat bedside. A tall, thin, worn-out-looking European guy in surgical scrubs barged in and said, "Is this the six-year-old that got sent for groceries and run over?" We were too surprised to respond as he continued. "I am the neurosurgeon and must examine her. Leave the room."

Jan was incensed as we reluctantly left. I was also fired up but chose not to respond. We returned a few minutes later as the neurosurgeon left without saying a word. I asked the nurse if she knew of the exam results; she did not. The nerve of this guy. He did not introduce himself, made an inaccurate comment, and left without letting us know the results of his exam. I promised myself not to let that happen again.

The phone started ringing with concerned relatives and friends. I fielded the calls as a young, blond social worker sat down with us and started asking lots of questions about Shannon and us. Visitors started to arrive. We were happy they were here but had little good news. All I said was that Shannon had had a good night.

Around noon the nurses were at work on Shannon's IV lines and other issues, so we adjourned to the meeting room we had now taken over. Jan's brothers had found a fried chicken joint nearby. I needed nourishment and started slamming spicy chicken. What a mistake as I sprinted for the restroom minutes later.

Late in the afternoon, I decided to hit the house and pick up some clothes, toys, and books for Shannon. We had gotten a room across the street at the Ronald McDonald House of New Jersey. I took the cell phone and told Jan to call me with any changes in Shannon's condition. I found my car and hit the highway, alone for the first time in thirty hours. My emotions exploded on the dashboard as I cried, sobbed, and groaned about the accident and Shannon's condition. Pain from stomach knots was unbearable. Buckets of tears blurred my vision as I managed to stay on the road. I prayed for Shannon's improvement and for the strength to drive on and control my emotions.

I started formulating a plan of rotating family members to watch Shannon. Jan and Tara would go to the Ronald McDonald House of Southern New Jersey at night while I stayed with Shannon. I would continue on the day shift as that was when the doctors checked Shannon and medical decisions were made. I would try to sleep at the House from 5:00 p.m. to 11:00 p.m. I reached out to my sisters and asked them to support us by visiting between 5:00 p.m. and 11:00 p.m. when I was not there.

I pulled into my driveway and parked the car as the adrenaline of yesterday returned with force. With my heart pounding and head spinning, I unlocked the door, afraid of facing a house without my healthy daughter running around. The family cat, ZZ Top (named after a guy from New York with a bad hairpiece), lunged at me with a thousand meows, demanding information. He seemed petrified. I had arranged with a neighbor to feed him. He was clearly alarmed at the isolation and Shannon's absence. I gave him a minute's attention and moved on.

I grabbed a suitcase and started tossing clothes in it. It was a surreal atmosphere, like I was watching everything on a big TV screen and not living it. If Shannon had been there, she would have, hilariously, followed me from room to room and jumped in the suitcase and hidden in the clothes. I finished packing by grabbing toiletries, then checked the answering machine. It was jammed with twenty-six messages from coworkers and friends I had grown up with. *My, how bad news travels fast.* My last stop was Shannon's playroom, where I grabbed about twenty books, five audio CDs, and a few stuffed animals. I also took down a framed picture of Shannon that I would post at her hospital bed. The breathing tube, adjacent ventilator, several IV lines, arterial line, and other medical devices all worked together to conceal Shannon's image. The picture would help all to recognize it was truly her. *Perhaps it would make some feel better as Shannon had been a healthy child and could return to that eventually.* I tossed everything in the car and took off back to the hospital. I was glad I did not see any neighbors as there was little good news to share.

I told myself to drive carefully with so many nuts on the road on July Fourth. As I approached the hospital exit, the highway shoulders had turned into a parking lot with hundreds of cars parking in order to catch the fireworks displays being conducted from the Delaware River. I arrived back at Cooper and was relieved there were no medical changes.

Jan and I immediately went to work posting the picture of Shannon above her bed, playing the CD from the Disney version of *Tarzan*, propping up the stuffed animals on her bed, and telling Shannon what books we had brought from home.

I sent the girls to the Ronald McDonald House for the night. The hospital security guard escorted them over. Armed with books and stuffed animals, I felt a surge of energy in the thirty-fourth hour. I started reading the books and voicing all of the characters. When I ran out of books, I made up stories using the stuffed animals. I continued with singing Shannon's favorite nursery rhymes. I am the world's worst singer but was not very self-conscious. I recalled reading somewhere years ago that people in comas can hear, and I sure hoped it was true. All of this verbal stimulation may help her feel more comfortable, I thought.

Parents of other kids in PICU started peering into our section. Nurses wondered where I got such energy. By 3:00 a.m. my voice was shot, so I grabbed two chairs, pulled them together to create a mini couch, and tried to rest in a horseshoe position. Shannon's monitors or the monitors of other patients went off constantly, so sleep was out of the question. I told myself to have some fresh material available when Shannon woke up and focused on that. I overheard the nurses take a call from Dr. Murza at 3:00 a.m. He had called to see how Shannon was doing. What dedication!

The nurse and respiratory tech made their usual rounds. Things were calm for a few hours until 4:00 a.m., when Shannon started arching her back like a drawbridge. The nurse took Shannon's temperature, which showed the fever had returned with a reading of 102 degrees. She gave Shannon an unscheduled dose of Tylenol and appeared to call the resident on duty. I resumed praying, putting the whole situation in God's hands. An exhausted-looking resident arrived and read Shannon's chart while listening to the nurse. Another young doctor arrived. They discussed Shannon's condition in medical terminology and decided to give her another medicine and a blood transfusion. I was jolted out of my seat by this turn of events and wanted an explanation. The resident calmly told me that Shannon's temperature was rising and her blood gases were not where we wanted them to be. It was not uncommon with brain injuries like this. My analytical ability was long gone in the fortieth hour. Shannon's posturing, rising temperature, and blood gases numbers were all bad signs.

The next temperature reading had increased to 104.6 degrees, and her heartbeat was almost 200 beats a minute. She continued arching her back and flailing her arms and legs. Her right arm started to tremble in what had to be a localized seizure. I did not know the seriousness of these signs, but the nurse did. She called the PICU resident back, who ordered an immediate CAT scan. "Immediate" was not very soon, as they had to assemble a transit team to escort Shannon to the CAT scan that included the PICU resident physician, the nurse, and a respiratory specialist. Shannon's fever came down to 102 degrees, and she was much calmer. The team must have given her more medication to prepare her for her trip to the CAT scan. Thank God, Jan and Tara arrived. I briefed them on the tough night, and they were angry I had not called them back to the hospital. I had thought about calling them but decided against it. They had witnessed the accident, and I thought an uninterrupted break might help them.

The transit team was set; they skillfully unhooked Shannon from the respirator machine and used a portable manually operated ventilator. They repositioned Shannon's IVs and transferred her to a smaller, more-mobile bed. Jan joined them on the elevator ride but was denied access to the CAT scan room. It turned out to be just as well because I later found out that just before the CAT scan, Shannon had had more local seizure activity in her right arm and had been given a higher dosage of the antiseizure medication Dilantin.

A close friend named Meg from Customs stopped by just as I needed some backup. She had hot coffee and fresh muffins and shared the story of her daughter's hospitalization last year with complex "stomach issues." Meg also asked for an article of Shannon's clothing to bring to the Padre Pio shrine nearby for prayer support. She had already briefed the entire Customs community on our situation and had taken the lead on coordinating all sorts of assistance. She had lots of hospital experience based on her daughter's stomach problems. Meg's visit was like that of a messenger angel, reviving our battered hopes after the difficult night.

Two hours later the team returned with Shannon and transferred her to the PICU bed with all attachments. CAT scans were taken of her head, neck, and stomach, and we were told doctors would discuss results with us, but the team did not seem alarmed. Shannon's temperature was back up to 103 degrees.

Visitors came and went all day. Their shocked faces upon seeing Shannon and all the connected apparatuses drove home the seriousness of the situation. Another chaplain stopped by and commented on Shannon's beauty upon seeing the eight-by-ten-inch photo above her bed. He led us in a prayer session. Nurses from the ER and social workers also stopped by. I was starting to tire out but found myself talking about Shannon's enthusiasm before the injury and how that would jump-start her recovery. The gruff foreign neurosurgeon stopped by; we had nicknamed him Dr. Cappuccino as that was much easier to pronounce than his longer last name.

"Please leave; I have to examine the patient."

"I'm not leaving. Yesterday your exam lasted thirty seconds, and you did not advise us or the nurse of the results. You still don't know her name. Dr. Murza keeps us informed. How about you do a joint exam with him?"

"I put results on the chart. I have to make rounds and have many patients to see." Dr. Cappuccino continued his hasty exam by calling Shannon, waiting for a response, looking at her pupils, and pushing her arms. "She won't wake up; she won't respond. The only thing she does is respond to a stimulus. I will order an MRI."

Dr. Cappuccino left. Jan and I were seething. I began wondering if this was the best hospital for my daughter. She deserved the best, and I had to provide it. Dr. Murza arrived and said he was waiting for the results of the CAT scan. He must have sensed our anger.

"It's good her fever is down. Since she has not woken up yet and has shown limited responses to a stimulus, she may have suffered a shearing injury. Such an injury involves a stretching or separation of neurons and axons in the brain that communicate messages. It can take several weeks to wake up from, and months to recover from, a shearing injury."

My sister the PT had brought up a shearing injury with the neurosurgeon on day one. It had sounded like a more hopeful diagnosis at the time, one that did not require surgery, but perhaps not if it was causing this coma.

First the fractures, then the bleeding and swelling in the brain, and now "shearing." This was not getting any easier. I buried my head in Shannon's bed and cried. Jan did the same for the next hour. My thirty-seventh birthday and Fourth of July celebrations were what I had been focused on two days ago. Now I was anchored to Shannon's bed, worried about her critical condition. I hoped and prayed that she was not feeling any pain. I kept picturing her waking up and being fine, just as victims in Hollywood movies emerge from comas.

More visitors from Customs arrived, promising to donate as much vacation time as I needed so that I could be with Shannon until she recovered. I was grateful for the visits and commitments of support and really needed some good news to spread. Dr. Murza seemed to feel the same way as he burst into our curtained-off bed.

"I just saw the CAT scans! There is no additional swelling or bleeding to the brain. It is virtually identical to the scan when she arrived. That is a great sign. The first forty-eight hours are when all bleeding and swelling occur and pressure increases within the skull. Bleeding and swelling rarely increase during the third twenty-four hours."

The day nurse was hovering beside Shannon like she was about to give some attention to the lines, tubes, and monitoring systems. Our visitors stayed beyond the curtain. I'm sure they did not want to interrupt anything and were struggling to hold it together. Many visitors knew Shannon as a healthy and energetic toddler. This had to be difficult.

My focus was on the continued monologue of Dr. Murza. "We'll do another scan in a few days, and I have scheduled an MRI for tomorrow. I anticipate it will indicate some bruising, which is what we expect. The cervical spine scan is clear, so we can remove the collar, and the stomach scan showed no sign of fluid. She must have had a tiny leak that sealed itself. Now if you will excuse me, I have to replace the arterial line that Shannon pulled out of her arm. This time I will insert it in the thigh area. That area is less mobile, and we will have an easier time drawing blood samples from it."

We were overjoyed by the good news. Our problems were rapidly being reduced. Shannon was alive, in critical but fairly stable condition, and she was communicating. We took the pulling out of the arterial line as a sign Shannon was in control of a small portion of her environment and had made a purposeful movement. I briefed the visitors and told them to spread the word that Shannon was improving.

The good news on Shannon's condition gave me more energy than eight hours of sleep would. I shared it with the parents of the other kids in the PICU and made some upbeat phone calls. Shannon's fever continued to fluctuate, spiking at 103 degrees. The nurses applied the air-conditioned blanket and cold compresses and adjusted medication after more consultation with doctors.

Evening rolled around, and Shannon's temperature had dropped to 101 degrees. I decided to maintain my scheduled rest at the Ronald McDonald House. It was right across the street from the hospital and provided room and board to the families of sick or injured children. Back in the 1970s and 1980s, every March, McDonald's restaurants in the Philadelphia area hosted a Shamrock Shake drive with all sales from those mint-flavored milkshakes going to the Ronald McDonald House of Philadelphia. That had been the extent of my contact with them.

I was impressed by the decorations of the New Jersey house. Joyful murals of kids playing outdoors in a scenic backdrop filled the walls, there were flowers on every table, and each room had some type of sports theme. The one we were in had a Philadelphia Flyers hockey team theme. I took my first shower in over two days and dreaded trying to fall asleep. I was exhausted after the fifty-plus-hour tear. The nausea and stomach-in-knots feelings would not let up.

I had gotten several cards from family members for my birthday. A half dozen nieces and nephews visited Shannon in the hospital and thought to give me a birthday card. I finally got a chance to open them and nearly giggled at the silly drawings of me engaging in horseplay with them, going back several years; I was surprised they remembered. They also interjected handwritten words of encouragement.

I relaxed enough to drift in and out of sleep. The routine was a half hour of sleep, then being jolted awake by thoughts of Shannon. I woke up to a nightmare, temporarily confused as to whether Shannon's condition was a scary dream or reality. I cried upon realizing the reality of our predicament and the fact that this was not something I could snap out of. I put the situation in God's hands, asking him to protect Shannon and restore her to health. After five hours of intermittent sleep, I got up and took another shower and headed back to Shannon's bedside.

The PICU was quieter at 11:00 p.m. Jan and Tara looked better than they had at any point in the last two days. They had assisted the nurse in giving Shannon a bath and washing her hair. Shannon looked better; her hair was neat, and some bruises were fading away. The girls left as I resumed my monologue of reading books, singing songs, and telling stories; my tone made it seem as though I had an audience of thousands.

Nurse Pat was running the PICU at midnight. I sensed she was the one who had gotten my wife to help with Shannon's bath. Last night she was skillfully in control of the PICU as she pumped the stomach of a twelve-year-old boy who had lost one leg and severely broken the other in a minibike accident. She had been frequently called to a four-year-old's bedside to advise other nurses how to treat a collapsed lung. She was in total command of the situation and projected an aura of confidence and enthusiasm. She must have had military experience based on her knowledge and organizational skills. She was tall and fit and definitely a knockout still today as in her younger days. Pat was becoming attached to Shannon like everyone else.

I stopped rambling at 3:00 a.m. and took a seat. Pat told me of patients with similar brain injuries who had recovered and of patients with less-serious head injuries who had done much worse than expected. She explained the two problems right now were the coma and spiking fevers. I had confidence in Pat and even more in Shannon.

At 4:30 a.m. Shannon's fever leveled off at 99 degrees, and Pat was in complete control. I could not get any rest in the rocking chair and suddenly found the confidence to crash in the conference room in the waiting area. I grabbed a few sheets and pillows from a hallway stash and hit the floor for an impressive two hours of rack time. I returned at 7:00 a.m., and Pat said Shannon's fever had gone back to 103 degrees but was now down to 100 degrees.

My brother Barry was already there for the first of his two daily visits. He briefed me on his discussions with insurance company reps. I updated him on the CAT scans and Shannon's fluctuating fevers. He seemed encouraged by her improving situation.

Jan and Tara returned, looking good as always due to their natural beauty but worn out. Nurse Pat stayed until 9:30 a.m., way past her shift. She gave the day nurse a long briefing on Shannon's ups and downs throughout the night. I went back to the Ronald McDonald House, took a shower, and got dressed in slacks and a suit jacket. I had decided to look sharp for all the professionals I was dealing with and to represent Shannon in style. This may sound like a reach, but we were grasping for answers at this stage. Could little things from fresh angles lead to surprising and improved results?

Back in the PICU, a team of doctors huddled around the nurse's station reviewing charts. They listened to Shannon's breathing and said she was doing a little better. They started to give Shannon liquid nutrition through an NG tube since she was unable to eat or drink. The trauma doctor was not someone we knew. The rotation of physicians was getting harder to figure out. A younger intern doctor usually led off, followed by a resident, and closing with an attending. They all listened to Shannon's breathing and reviewed or wrote in the charts. The trauma attending doctor asked why an antibiotic had been prescribed for Shannon. Dr. Murza resumed his perfect timing by arriving and answering the question immediately, stating he had ordered it as a precaution against pneumonia setting in. The trauma doctor said it was too early for such an infection. Dr. Murza said a trace of the bacteria that form pneumonia had been present in a blood test. They agreed to maintain the antibiotic.

Nothing like being hit by another ton of bricks. "Pneumonia!" I knew of several older people who had gone into the hospital with this infection and never come back. It made sense since Shannon could not cough up mucus. The respiration tech came by every hour and suctioned it out. One more thing to put in God's hands.

Shannon's PT stopped by and did lots of ranging of her arms and legs. Jan and I rotated talking to Shannon and fielding phone calls from concerned friends and relatives. This was becoming a distraction. I made a mental note to come up with a way to limit them. The transport team arrived on schedule to take Shannon for the MRI. We could not accompany her per hospital policy. Over three hours later, they returned saying the MRI had had technical problems and they had given Shannon medicine to sedate her and keep her still due to her agitated state. They had no results yet as a radiological neurologist had to review them. The PICU was busy with patients and visitors.

Dr. Cappuccino stopped by with a young Indian intern who had to be in training. Before he could leave, we asked him about the MRI results.

"No, I have not seen the MRI. I am still looking for the CAT scan from yesterday. They lose things around here. I told her to find it," he said as he motioned to the intern. "All the MRI will show is what I already know, some bruising."

Thank God he left right away as we were incensed by his lack of interest in my daughter's condition and the results of tests. I wondered if sounding off like an irate customer would help. I needed answers, and there was no sense of urgency from the expert. I had to focus on my daughter's condition and what was best for her. Was it time to get her to a more specialized hospital for her condition?

I joined Jan and Tara in the conference room with one of my sisters. We talked and decided to move Shannon to the best brain injury recovery facility we could find. I had my sisters already looking into facilities in the region. Now was the time to visit them.

Dr. Murza returned to Shannon's bed and said he had seen the MRI results and would brief us on the findings. The nurses must have seen the veins bulging from my neck and called him. Jan and I sat down next to Shannon, with Tara and two of my sisters standing close by. Dr. Murza came in and closed the curtain, all that separated beds and patients in the PICU. He started by apologizing for the confusion on scan results and the ill-mannered Dr. Cappuccino. Jan blew off some steam describing our recent encounters. Dr. Murza said that was not acceptable and he would follow up with the hospital administration.

Dr. Murza had Jan and I sit down as he did the same and started a long discourse. "I have seen the MRI films, and they do show some bruising. Yesterday's CAT scan showed no additional swelling or bleeding, which is good, but Shannon has yet to wake up. She has suffered what is called diffuse axon injury."

I was experiencing an indescribable feeling of nauseous burning.

"That is a shearing or tearing of the neurons and axons. The brain transmits messages through the connected axons. Children as young as Shannon have brains that are capable of rewiring themselves and sending messages through different pathways. I think Shannon will be in a coma for three or four weeks, then she will be hospitalized for three or four months recovering from this injury."

An ice-cold feeling ran through my veins, and I started shivering as Dr. Murza kept talking. "I am basing this on the hundreds of brain injuries I have seen. Shannon's pupil response is brisk, and her reaction to stimulus is strong. I could be wrong, but my gut feeling is Shannon will be one of the kids that recovers and playfully hides behind her parents on a return visit."

I grabbed a rolled-up sheet from the bottom of Shannon's bed and wrapped it around my shoulders as I reached for Jan. She was white as a ghost but did not seem to be shivering like me.

Dr. Murza was undeterred by our reactions and continued his overwhelming briefing. "There are three brain injury rehab facilities we recommend. Children's Hospital of Philadelphia; Bancroft in Voorhees; not far from here, and DuPont Hospital for Children in Wilmington, Delaware. We have sent many kids to DuPont, and they have done well."

Dr. Murza flawlessly shifted from talk of facilities to Shannon's treatment plan.

"We will start to reduce the amount of oxygen on Shannon's ventilator and hope to wean her off it completely by late next week. She should be ready to be moved to rehab in three weeks."

I noticed two of my sisters, identical twins, close by; they had heard all this and were not looking very good. Their eyes appeared glassy as one ran for water to prevent the other from fainting. They found chairs just in time.

"Is she in a life-threatening situation?" I found the strength to ask a question.

"If she develops pneumonia, she will be."

"What is the process for transferring her?"

"It is coordinated by social workers here and at the rehab facility. Doctors and nurses talk to each other, and a transport team will move her, most likely in a ground ambulance. If you want to move her earlier, let me know and we will make it happen."

Dr. Murza had provided answers and outlined the start of a recovery plan, but we were beyond devastated with this lengthy hospital stay and recovery process. We were expecting Shannon to wake up at any minute. Three to four more weeks of this torture—how would we survive? It was going to be a long battle. I had to stay active.

Jan had ripped me for not bringing more essential supplies from the house, so I decided to make a run with her now since my sisters were watching Shannon. I told Shannon we would be right back as we left, and Shannon raised her arm and waved. It was most likely an involuntary muscle contraction, but I chose to believe that Shannon could hear us and had responded.

We rushed home. Jan froze in front of the house. She faced the same chilling emotions I had two days ago, of the house without Shannon. Several neighbors spotted us and rushed to provide support. They stayed with Jan as I grabbed the remaining essentials. I coldly gave the family cat to one neighbor. I gave the house keys to another neighbor with instructions to retrieve the mail and water the plants. We ate a healthy dinner at another neighbor's house. It was a productive but agonizing trip home.

We returned two hours later and found my sisters Betty and Patty getting along wonderfully with Nurse Pat. They were swapping stories of growing up as identical twins as Nurse Pat, too, was a twin. We relieved the sisters and hung out with Shannon, her fevers still spiking.

Jan and Tara left around midnight for the Ronald McDonald House. Kowoski from Customs arrived, as I had requested some backup for the midnight ride. He was encouraged by Shannon's improved appearance. Pat managed to contain Shannon's fever to under 102 degrees, and I sent Kowoski home at 3:30 a.m.

Nurse Pat and I talked for an hour. She suggested I crash in the conference room, and I was happy to oblige. I found out later she had arranged with hospital security to not question my use of the room after hours. What a nurse! At 7:30 a.m. the girls were back, as well as Barry, who had already heard from Pat that Shannon had had a good night. Thank God! The reduced fever, a few hours of sleep, a supportive family, and an optimistic PICU attending physician had given me a surge of energy. The weekend had arrived. It was time to do some reconnaissance on the brain injury rehab facilities Dr. Murza had suggested.

The hospital OT stopped by and could not get a hand brace on Shannon's wrist. She said that she was filling in and did not work with children. I told her to leave it for my PT sister to put on and decided to move up my Monday recons to now. My sister Anne arrived and took a few seconds to apply the brace by elevating Shannon's thumb.

She joined me on a visit to the Children's Hospital of Philadelphia (CHOP). We had no appointment, but a nursing supervisor understood our situation and gave us a tour of their gigantic PICU. It consisted of forty rooms, twenty on each side. Families were everywhere watching over their sick infants. All seemed very proficient and a little overwhelming. CHOP was world-renowned for treating children with all types of cancer. They had a brain injury rehab section called the Seashore House. I asked about the Ronald McDonald House of Philadelphia and learned it was only available to families from outside the commuting area. The nursing supervisor told us she could coordinate moving Shannon as early as tonight. It was a great facility with lots of resources.

My coworker Surfer joined me for the midnight ride and was impressed that Shannon's bruises were fading away and the cervical collar was gone. Having friends present sure helped to pass the painful hours. He brought cards from the Customs community and further promises of leave donation if I needed it. I had over four months of annual and sick leave and hoped that would be more than enough. We talked about the twists and turns of life and how you never knew what was around the corner. Nurse Pat was present, so I sent Surfer home at 3:30 a.m. and got a few hours' sleep in the conference room.

On Sunday morning I drove to DuPont Hospital for Children in Wilmington, Delaware, which is thirty-five miles from Cooper. Anne met me there. We did not have an appointment but found another gracious nursing supervisor who gave us a tour. The PICU was smaller than CHOP's, with twenty rooms. They were separated by glass, which was better than curtains. We also saw the rehab wing where patients recovering from brain injury stayed. Therapy schedules were posted that detailed six to eight hours of daily activity per patient. We learned of DuPont's long history of treating brain injuries. The hospital setting was paradise compared to Camden, with rolling hills, beautifully landscaped gardens, and blooming trees. We also visited the Ronald McDonald House of Delaware; they would allow us to stay there with less restriction on how close we lived. I did not want the hassle of commuting back and forth from Shannon to an empty house. Anne had done some research on the medical staff and found the top neurosurgeon in the area was in charge at DuPont. I was convinced that DuPont was the best place for Shannon.

I rushed back to Cooper and enthusiastically briefed my wife and daughter on DuPont. I advised Dr. Murza on the decision, and he said he would make it happen by tomorrow. We were relieved to have made this decision and felt in greater control of the situation. Such decisions are not easy when you're dealing with the stress of a daughter in critical condition. The social worker and nurses did the necessary coordination, and the insurance company approved the move.

I spent our final night at Cooper accompanied by another Customs coworker. His name was Zach, and he was an avid smoker. He spent four hours with me without taking a cigarette break. A few doctors checked in, saying DuPont was a great place. Dr. Cappuccino kept his distance. A psychologist stopped by and encouraged us to talk about the accident. I got the impression Dr. Cappuccino had referred us to him. The psychologist urged me to take medication to remain calm based on the stress he could see on my face. I told him I would consider it.

On Monday morning I packed the car, and we were all set to leave for DuPont. The regular PICU PT stopped by and apologized for the weekend services. My sister Anne had left word with her to check Shannon's wrist for a fracture. The PT took a long look at it and ordered x-rays, which were positive for a fracture. An orthopedic surgeon set and cast the wrist right in the PICU and said DuPont may perform surgery. Shannon was still in her coma and heavily medicated to reduce the brain swelling, so no anesthesia was necessary. She was not even aware of the new cast. How could the hospital have missed this? Another good reason to move to DuPont.

The transport team arrived from DuPont and got a full briefing from the Cooper PICU nurses on IV bags, medications, and ventilator settings. One nurse worked the manual airbag as Shannon was placed on the ambulance stretcher. She said Shannon was doing most of the breathing herself and was requiring infrequent manual pushes of oxygen.

The day nurses hugged the stuffing out of us and handed the transport team a stack of Shannon's medical records. I gave my contact information to the nurses and other parents of patients and promised to report back on Shannon's progress. There had been about six other patients throughout the week in the PICU. A few had come and only stayed a few hours. One family had stood by their twelve-year-old son, as he had lost his leg in a quad accident. Another family had a four-year-old son with a skull fracture and severely bruised face from a fall. I did not speak much to them, but Jan did and provided frequent support by listening to them and sharing our fear of Shannon's injuries. Still, I felt like I knew them as they had watched my speeches to Shannon most of the week and seemed to wonder where I had gotten such energy.

I thanked the nurses and was sad Nurse Pat was not present. We went down to the ambulance and were told none of us could ride with Shannon. A PICU nurse ran to our car with a copy of Shannon's wrist x-ray. We followed the ambulance and dealt with the return of nauseous stomachs and tingling spines as Shannon was still in a coma after one week and back on the road on medical transport.

It felt good to leave Cooper for a more specialized brain injury treatment facility. I learned by the end of the week that the interns had started on July

1, which was the national intern start date. Their lack of familiarity must have caused some of the confusion. Hopefully Shannon would be more comfortable in the pediatric hospital, and prompt therapy would spark her to wake up. The ER team, PICU nurses, and Dr. Murza did a great job in treating Shannon during the golden hour and the first week. The struggles with some physicians and therapists and the difficulty in getting results were behind us.

The ride to DuPont took us over several bridges and south on Interstate 95. The traffic was light, and the ambulance did not need to use its lights and siren. We were still worried sick about Shannon but confident our big decision would jump-start her recovery.

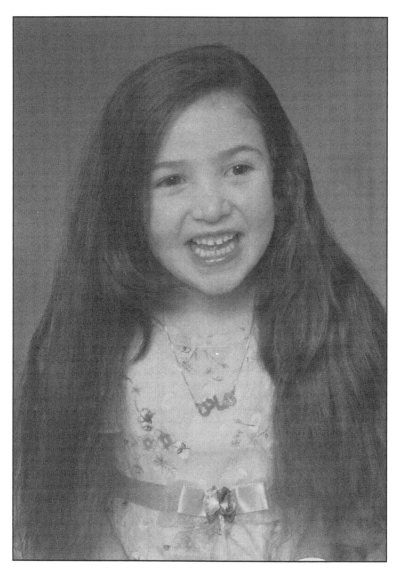

The picture of Shannon we posted by her bed in the PICU

3

ANOTHER DOSE OF PESSIMISM

We pulled into the ER right behind the ambulance. Jan got out of the car and joined Shannon on the way to the PICU. It only took me a few seconds to find a parking spot in the gigantic lot surrounded by majestic scenery of rolling hills and tall trees. Tara and I joined Jan in the PICU, where Shannon was already resting in a private room with the vital sign readers connected to a monitor, her IVs set, and the respirator connected. A doctor who Jan identified as a PICU resident was examining Shannon. Dr. Narajavo was a tall, well-spoken guy with a darker complexion who dressed comfortably and appeared to be in his early thirties.

"I'm Dr. Narajavo, the chief resident here. We're glad you chose DuPont for your daughter. My discussions with the doctors at Cooper and the brief exam I just did indicate that Shannon most likely has a significant shearing injury. The neurologist and neurosurgeon will be here shortly to see her."

The PICU resident seemed really on the ball and ready to lead the charge on Shannon's recovery. Hopefully everyone here was just as squared away. He continued to articulate the game plan.

"I have also ordered a consult with an orthopedic surgeon since they just discovered her broken wrist today. I have ordered a full series of x-rays for our evaluation. Shannon can't tell us if she is in pain anywhere. We'll evaluate the records from Cooper, discuss our findings here, and come up with a treatment plan."

I noticed that another doctor who had to be the neurologist had already started his exam of Shannon. He was wearing a suit, so I doubted he was a surgeon. Dr. Narajavo continued his spiel on the treatment plan. "We are planning on extubating her, or removing her breathing tube, tomorrow. The ventilator numbers indicate she is doing most of the breathing work herself. This recovery will be a long and slow process. I'll be talking to you more tomorrow morning."

Dr. Narajavo walked toward the nurses' station, and I overheard him give instructions to call everyone on duty together so he could update them on their new patient. We went into Shannon's room, where Dr. Bowman, the neurologist, was at work. He had a black doctors' bag dating back to the 1960s and an even older flashlight. He used the flashlight to check Shannon's pupil response. He clapped a few times, trying to startle Shannon to respond. He wrapped up the exam and gave us the results.

"There are two main parts of the brain, the brain stem, which controls breathing and the eyes, and the hemispheres, which control motor and cognitive skills. The brain stem appears to be intact, but the hemispheres are severely injured. Shannon's most severe injury, that of the diffuse axons, is one that we don't see on x-ray or CAT scan images."

I noticed Dr. Narajavo was briefing ten to fifteen employees at the nurses' station. He appeared to be giving direct instructions on labs and x-rays he wanted to be completed as soon as possible. This immediate implementation of action was reassuring as Dr. Bowman continued to break our hearts.

Dr. Bowman continued, "You evaluate such an injury by watching the patient. There is no way to determine when she will wake up or to what extent she can recover. With a brain injury of this magnitude, we don't know if Shannon will make a full recovery or if she will ever do more than she is doing now."

I noticed another doctor reviewing images of Shannon's brain in a mounted light box and discussing them with another doctor. Both wore surgical scrubs. One had to be Dr. FitzPatrick, the highly recommended neurosurgeon. Dr. Bowman wrapped up his comments with a glimpse of hope. "I have seen amazing things happen in rehab, and hopefully Shannon will be one of those children. I will order an electroencephalogram (EEG) scan on Shannon's brain, which will show us more details of what areas of her brain are damaged. That will be done tomorrow right in this room. I will talk to you after I have the results."

Nauseousness had become my constant companion, so there was no danger of collapsing despite this grim outlook. The girls did not look good. We turned our attention to Dr. FitzPatrick. He had an authentic British accent and looked a little worn out, probably due to a day of performing surgery. He and his associate did a joint exam on Shannon. They had a female staff member join them. Nothing could have prepared us for the results.

"I'm Dr. FitzPatrick, and this is Dr. Graham. He works with me. This is my nurse practitioner, Kim Stevens. We just examined Shannon and reviewed the charts from Cooper, and I am sorry to inform you that Shannon has a severe traumatic brain injury, not mild, not moderate, but severe. She has two skull fractures, which are probably causing her body temperature to fluctuate so greatly. She has a subdural hematoma, meaning a small amount of hemorrhaging in the brain, which is forcing her muscles to have so much spasticity."

Wow, this guy is providing detail I did not hear at Cooper, but it is all negative. How can I stop him? His facial expression was serious and grim. His comments did indicate he was the foremost neurosurgeon in the region.

Dr. FitzPatrick continued to demonstrate his expertise by stating, "The swelling in her brain is quite significant. I am most concerned about her shearing injury. Her MRI shows global shearing of neurons and axons throughout the brain. The outerlying axons are somewhat resistant to brain injury in terms of damaging brain function. The axons in the midbrain and deeper are not resistant to injury and indicate long-term consequences."

Jan and Tara were hysterical and on the verge of passing out. They were already sitting at a table outside Shannon's room, so I was not worried about them falling. I had to stop this barrage of negative information as chills ran up my spine. Time to speak up.

"Shannon is only three years old. Doesn't she have a great chance of waking up soon and recovering?"

"Age is in her favor, but I would not expect her to wake up for weeks, and the severity of her brain injuries makes significant recovery fairly unrealistic."

"How do you know this? By reviewing the scans?"

Like I had any foundation of knowledge to question the expert who was using medical terminology and injury descriptions like it was a normal routine.

"Yes, the scans, charts from Cooper, and my exam all indicate the severity of her injuries. I'll be checking on her every day. I know you are in a state of shock, but try to get some rest. She will need your support when she wakes up and starts the therapy regimen."

Both doctors shook our hands and left. A portable x-ray technician arrived to take lots more pictures. A nurse drew several tubes of blood. We were devastated, having felt some comfort arriving at the Emerald City (DuPont) only to find the Great Oz (Dr. FitzPatrick) had no magic to heal Shannon. We had to find another yellow-brick road, so I told Jan we would go get checked in at the Ronald McDonald House of Delaware and Tara would watch Shannon. Jan remained hysterical as we drove across the street to the newer building on the spectacular grounds.

We had grown dependent on the optimism of Dr. Murza and now felt like we had been sledgehammered off a cliff. I brought up how much more organized DuPont seemed to be. We drove the short distance to the Ronald McDonald House of Delaware and barely noticed the lush landscape or rolling hills.

There was a large mansion on adjacent grounds where some of the DuPont family members lived. They owned a large company that provided materials to industries worldwide. Alfred I. DuPont had opened the hospital in nearby Wilmington in 1940, and it had since become renowned for excellence in pediatric orthopedics. The current hospital was completed in 1984 and enjoyed an excellent reputation for treating all pediatric medical conditions.

The Ronald McDonald House of Delaware looked modern and impressive from the outside. There was ample parking and a bench with a full lifelike figure of Ronald McDonald smiling to greet all visitors. An elderly house employee completed our check-in procedures. She gave us a briefing, provided us with linens and towels, and explained mealtimes. We could not focus on any of this. The employee, who was probably an unpaid volunteer, continued to ignore my bawling wife and gave us a quick tour of the house, including the laundry room and downstairs gym. It finally ended, and we collapsed in our room and held each other. Where would we find the energy to stay strong and upbeat for Shannon while facing this complex and difficult diagnosis?

Eventually I went to get the bags from the car. When I returned, Jan was crying in front of the house social worker, named Marge. Marge introduced herself as the family advocate of the house. I gave her a quick synopsis of Shannon's condition. She promised to visit Shannon tomorrow and encouraged us to meet another parent staying in the house with a daughter who had suffered a brain injury similar to Shannon's. I guess our tour guide had noticed Jan's hysterics. I was grateful she'd followed up. Marge was helpful and very sharp.

Marge left, and within minutes that parent she wanted us to meet knocked on the door. She introduced herself as Joanne and was eager to share her story. There must be a natural bond between the parents of brain-injured children. Perhaps one day I could help parents deal with this painful nightmare, which had to be tougher for the injured children. Her daughter had been struck by a pickup truck last summer while operating a lemonade stand on the sidewalk and had not been expected to survive. She was in a coma for thirty days and had made remarkable progress but was not walking or talking yet. Joanne gave us a book that covered the basics of brain injury and promised to visit Shannon in the morning as well.

Meeting Marge and Joanne gave us the second wind to return to the hospital. Their willingness to support and share with people they had just met minutes before was impressive. Time to get back to Shannon and Tara, who had to be exhausted. Tara reported that Shannon had been given a high dose of Dilantin since a blood test indicated she was very low on this antiseizure drug. She also said an orthopedic surgeon had stopped by to check Shannon's wrist and said a three-year-old can recover from such a brain injury. This made me recall when Dr. Murza at Cooper said such a brain injury would leave no hope for recovery in an adult, but since toddlers' brains were pliable, they could recover from such an injury. I told myself to remember what Dr. Murza had said and forget what Dr. FitzPatrick had said. *Anything to keep going and find some hope in this sea of negativity.*

I resumed my one-way conversations with Shannon with more enthusiasm than ever. I congratulated her on doing so well on the ambulance ride and described her new room in fine detail. I elaborated about the beautifully landscaped hospital grounds and told her of walks around the hospital we would take looking at birds, squirrels, and rabbits. The glass partitions afforded much more privacy than the curtains in the Cooper PICU. I could really sound off without the other parents staring at me. I again noticed Dr. Narajavo at the nurses' station coordinating the treatment of Shannon with a dozen hospital employees such as nurses, PTs, respiratory technicians, and x-ray technicians. It felt good to be in this facility that specialized in treating children and was forming a detailed treatment plan.

Tara volunteered to spend the night with Shannon. Jan and I returned to the Ronald McDonald House, took sleeping pills, and crashed. Each of us was jolted awake in a cold sweat several times throughout the night from the realization that we were living a nightmare.

We were still in a state of shock the next morning. My dad and sister Anne visited. I shared with them the heavy doses of pessimism we had received upon arrival. Anne got right to work ranging Shannon's limbs. My dad took me to the cafeteria for an early lunch. He suggested I return to work as it may take my mind off the situation and enable me to save leave time for when Shannon was awake and undergoing therapy. My sister Pat visited with a van full of Gatorade. I had still not been able to hold down food, and the Gatorade was my only source of nourishment for the next month. It sure helped to have a great family at a time like this.

The brain scan was done early Tuesday morning, and Dr. Bowman provided almost instant results of some bruising throughout the brain but not in the brain stem or in an area that would cause Shannon to have seizures. I took that as good news and did not ask any questions. Doctor and therapist visits started early and lasted all day, with the entire rehab staff stopping by. Their department was Shannon's next destination once she was awake and could participate in therapy sessions. The sooner we made that transition, the better. The PICU PT ranged Shannon's limbs just as Anne had been doing and conferred with Anne on treatment of Shannon's inverted feet and hands. Anne was impressed with this therapist's knowledge and aggressive approach to posturing. Things were looking up again.

I had seen about half of the other patients in the PICU, and spasticity seemed to be a common problem, especially with kids in wheelchairs due to cerebral palsy. It is a symptom associated with damage to the brain, spinal cord, and motor nerves. It results in muscle tightness due to muscle contraction over a long duration. Many of the kids had foot or arm braces, and therapists were doing the same ranging activities with them. Other kids were facing organ transplants. Their color and body shape looked unhealthy. A few kids had no parents present. Imagine having to tackle these medical challenges without family support.

Jan and Tara got to know other parents quickly. Females clearly form bonds more easily and need to talk about situations. Most of the parents had more familiarity with intensive care units and medical conditions as they had been here before. The kids who had cerebral palsy seemed to average a surgery per summer. When a parent was a donor to their baby in need of an organ transplant, the person was quite busy doing double duty as patient and parent.

I found myself completing quick recons of the hospital so I knew where the cafeteria was. I still could not hold down food, but I could tell visitors where it was. I also marked the chapel, gift shop, surgical wing, rehab wing (our much-desired destination), casting room, imaging section, child activities room, and the basement floor with a physician library, weight room for employees, basketball court (currently covered with wheelchairs), and pool for PT. When frustrated, I would bolt on a quick recon and try to find satisfaction in the latest destination within the hospital I had located and visualized showing it to Shannon when she was awake, alert, and comfortable enough for a full hospital tour. The basement had a real incline on one end that I thought would be fun to ride down when Shannon was back in her stroller.

At 2:00 p.m. Dr. Narajavo and a couple of residents and nurses joined forces to perform the extubation on Shannon. Dr. Narajavo talked the group through his actions, but all his focus was on Shannon.

"Come on, big girl, we need to see your beautiful face. Try to blow out, and I will pull for a few seconds. You'll feel much better."

Dr. Narajavo pulled with two hands, and the tube was out as Shannon made a few groaning sounds to celebrate.

Yes! Shannon had been successfully weaned off the ventilator and was breathing on her own. The nurse gave us swabs to wash out Shannon's mouth with, and she reminded us this was another step in a long process. With the breathing tube gone and Shannon's bruises just about gone, she looked more like her healthy self. For the first time in eight days, we could hold her on our laps and hug her. Holding her was like a dream come true.

I sat in the rocking chair next to the bed and resumed reading books to Shannon with more energy than ever.

On Wednesday morning two PICU PTs were the first of a parade of specialists. Shannon was no longer attached to a breathing tube, so they gave her as rigorous a workout as was possible for someone in a coma. They got her up on a large gym ball and spun her around in a way that exerted pressure on her muscles. This put direct pressure on Shannon's limbs, which she needed as she was not conscious to do it herself. The PT's confidence and command of techniques offset the fear we felt watching Shannon get twirled around like a spinning top.

Next, we headed down to the casting room, where the technicians had even more enthusiasm. They spoke to Shannon like she was wide awake, promising to provide her first choice in cast colors. I had taken a seat in the casting room, feeling despondent over Shannon's condition and the overwhelming pessimism of so many physicians. Every few hours such feelings of despair and sadness surfaced and were difficult to chase away. The PICU PT continued to talk to Shannon with incredible enthusiasm.

"Are you opening your eyes?"

I got out of the chair like a shot and saw Shannon actually blink a few times. She seemed to be listening to the PT. *Awesome!* We had another magnificent sign straight from Shannon. *Wait until I tell the pessimists upstairs about this.* Shannon had recognized I was down and sent the perfect sign to encourage me. The rigorous PT session had clearly paid off.

The PT massaged Shannon's feet to get them as straight as possible. A cast technician then applied the wet bandages full of plaster to make the casts. They topped it off with pink tape. I promptly wrote, "Dad Loves Shannon." The cast technicians and PT seemed to be as uplifted as I was.

Shannon's next stop was the rehab-wing gym. I decided to go work on some administrative issues with hospital billing as I had been putting them off since we arrived. I was glad that my brother had handled the first weeks' worth of administrative duties. It was time for me to get more involved.

We were fortunate to have decent auto and health insurance and would be drawing on both to cover all these hospital expenses. Jan stayed with Shannon through her second PT session.

I returned an hour later, and Jan gloriously reported Shannon had opened her left eye several times on a repeat exercise of spinning on the large gym ball. We were ecstatic with this sign from Shannon and knew it was a message that big things were on the way.

Back in the PICU room, Dr. Bowman stopped by after hearing Shannon had opened her eyes. He asked Shannon to repeat the feat for him, but she remained unresponsive. He remarked on Shannon looking different the last three days, a little better each time.

"Shannon has had a big couple of days, with arriving here, getting off the ventilator, and opening her eyes briefly. Shortly she will be discharged from intensive care to rehab. Her appearance has improved, but you need to get accustomed to her not making such progress. She will plateau, then make progress, then plateau again. She may not open her eyes again until next week."

What a negative summation of events that we had found extraordinary. *Shannon has given us a surge of hope for the first time in nine days, and this guy is suppressing it. We will choose to stay positive and see further progress. He did say she would move to the rehab unit.* We checked with the nurse, who confirmed Shannon was being discharged from the PICU and moving to rehab. We packed all the books, videotapes, and gifts Shannon had received from visitors and departed the PICU. It only took one nurse to transport her across the hospital. I made a promise to the PICU nurses that Shannon would walk back here to visit them in a few months. They smiled and must have been thinking that I did not know what a long shot that was.

The PICU PT's last official act was to outfit Shannon with a wheelchair. It was waiting for us in Shannon's new room in rehab. We strapped Shannon in it and carefully secured her head, which would fall freely to her chest if left unsupported. Seeing Shannon in a wheelchair was another devastating moment that lasted a few minutes. We rejoiced at the opportunity to take her for walks. We walked Shannon around the rehab wing several times as she remained unresponsive. I gave her a sparkling description of the area, including painted pictures on walls of playful pets and other kids residing here. Some had visible illnesses; some did not.

We walked into the rehab gym, and four therapists greeted Shannon as if she were wide awake. They knew she was their new patient and were at work devising a routine for her based on the PICU PT's report, which they had just read. Their enthusiasm and dedication made a lasting impression.

The rehab wing was full of patients recovering from brain injury or suffering from cerebral palsy. Several infants with neurological issues were there with their parents, who looked like they had been through the wringer. A three-year-old girl with a badly broken leg was in the room next to Shannon's. She had been in a car accident that had been fatal for four out of six occupants. Teenagers recovering from falls off bicycles or skateboards were walking around looking completely healthy, but they had severe cognitive deficits. The poor kids with cerebral palsy were confined to wheelchairs and had trouble speaking and moving their limbs freely. In the room across from Shannon, there was a fourteen-year-old boy from the United Arab Emirates recovering from surgery to both knees to straighten out his legs. He clearly had cognitive challenges as well. His dad, Ramsey, was with him and spoke no English. He patrolled the hallway in his native Middle Eastern garb and greeted people in Arabic.

We settled Shannon back in her room as the evening nurse placed a feeding tube in Shannon's nose to get her some nutrition. That was better than receiving nourishment via IV lines. Shannon's breathing tube was gone, but her breathing seemed unnatural. She could not spit out mucus. Doctors ordered breathing treatments for her that involved a respiratory tech putting a tube in her mouth and pumping in medicated air. The respiratory techs were the same ones who had tended to her in the PICU and commented on how much better Shannon looked. Shannon's hand was connected to a pulse ox monitor that read 90 percent, so she was breathing OK without ventilator support. Shannon's temperature had stabilized over the past few days. She was getting a new medicine for blood pressure, which helped control the fevers. She was still on heavy doses of Dilantin to prevent seizures.

I went to the hospital chapel and thanked God for all the positive developments. Previous trips to the chapel had been eventful as I had started in the kneeling position and ended up prone on the pad crying about Shannon's condition and hoping she could not feel much pain. Today was the first time I remained upright. I was able to keep my emotions in check in front of my family but lost it when isolated in the chapel.

On this chapel call, I thanked God for saving Shannon from death; for enabling us to move her to DuPont; for her rapid progress since arriving—breathing tube removal, some eye openings; and for the team of professionals that was taking charge. I prayed for the strength to provide the support Shannon needed. I knew my family members were praying constantly and was confident rapid progress was on the way based on their close relationship with God.

It was a relief to let emotions out. I returned to Shannon's room refreshed and ready to read her more books and tell stories. Ramsey would drift in and out of our room hoping my wife and sister-in-law would welcome him. He would stare at me like he was waiting for compliments on his garments. I would continue reading to the unresponsive Shannon. She was posturing less and not as uncomfortable in bed.

Dr. FitzPatrick, the renowned neurosurgeon, maintained his daily visits even though Shannon was out of the PICU and not a surgical patient. He was encouraged by the reduction of spasticity in Shannon's muscles and her more stable temperatures. He spoke of the importance of Shannon eventually showing purposeful movements. Maybe he had some Oz magic after all.

The orthopedic surgeon stopped by to check Shannon's fractured wrist. He was shocked that Shannon had pulled the wrist out of alignment in the cast that they had set at Cooper. That seemed like a deliberate response to me. Shannon had had the strength to yank her broken wrist from the rigid plaster, or her movement was a sign of agitation at her serious condition. He called a few interns and made them watch as he set a new cast all the way up her arm and over her elbow so she could not displace it again. Shannon did look uncomfortable in three casts. She continued to thrash in the bed at times and started to audibly groan. This had to be a sign she was working to get better.

Shannon's nurse in rehab was a veteran named Mary. Mary made herself the point of contact for all physicians, therapists, and technicians, which took the load off of us. Mary was in her early forties, petite, with short black hair and an amazing level of enthusiasm. She made plans and took immediate action. Within two days she removed the catheter and had Shannon wearing diapers. She also removed the arterial line, treated the sores it left behind, and switched the IV lines to Shannon's other arm. She showed us lots of ways to make Shannon more comfortable by adjusting her pillows and changing her body position. The prayers I mentioned earlier were being answered by an angel named Nurse Mary.

Tara was now spending nights with Shannon. She would return to the hospital at 7:00 p.m. looking sharp, all dressed up and happy to spend time with Shannon. Jan and I would return to the Ronald McDonald House and try to help each other sleep with little success.

The parade of doctors continued over the next few days. Some were concerned about Shannon's blood pressure and considered applying a patch to Shannon's arm to deliver medicine. Another doctor was worried about her liver being out of position and ordered an immediate ultrasound. Another doctor explained they would dye the food that the NG tube was delivering to see if she could digest it properly. I sensed Shannon was the celebrity patient and all wanted to join her team, which was not a bad thing. The ultrasound turned out fine.

The attending physician in the rehab wing became our go-to person, as she explained everything in plain language and encouraged all to give Shannon more time to rest. She also told us we had to find a way to rest and suggested weekly counseling sessions with the social worker on staff.

Visitors continued, bringing all sorts of cards and stuffed animals for Shannon. Many had visited her at Cooper, and all were impressed with the improvements. Joanne, whom we met upon checking in at Ronald McDonald House of Delaware, and her two daughters visited. Her older daughter was the one from the car accident and looked OK despite being in a wheelchair and not speaking. Her younger daughter, who was about three years old, sang an entire Britney Spears song for Shannon and gave her heart-shaped hair ribbons. She had clearly learned a lot through her sister's ordeal. Joanne said that Shannon was much stronger than her daughter had been at this stage despite still being in a coma.

My brother Barry visited, and a senior hospital anesthesiologist stopped by to see him. Barry had defended him on a malpractice case at CHOP. The anesthesiologist was very glad Shannon's breathing tube had been removed, as needing it any longer would have required a tracheostomy tube to be placed in her throat.

The three of us talked in the hallway, then walked into the room where Shannon was playing peekaboo with Jan. She would open one eye, close it, and then open the other one for a few seconds. *Yes! More blinking. Where the hell was Dr. Bowman?*

We played Disney tapes nonstop for Shannon. During the *Peter Pan* movie, she resumed blinking her eyes and seemed to be trying to watch Tinker Bell spread angel dust.

The recent change in her fever medication was effective, as Shannon finally enjoyed a day without a fever. Her blood pressure had also improved.

Shannon seemed to become more aware and more restless. She started to groan and wheeze and thrust her arms about in a frustrated way. Jan got right in bed with her and was able to calm her down. I made an audio tape of my usual material (stories and books) for Shannon so Tara could play it at night when I was not there. I remembered Nurse Pat at Cooper saying agitation would increase as Shannon got more alert. We had come a long way in a short time and were eager to tackle such agitation.

On Saturday morning the hospital was deserted. Shannon's fever had returned Friday night, and she was very restless. She must not have been able to tell the difference between night and day. The orthopedic surgeon stopped by to check Shannon's wrist again, and we welcomed him as he was the resident optimist. He was wearing an army uniform that sported a colonel's rank. He explained he would be reporting to weekend reserve duty today. I shared my army officer background, and Dr. White gave me a short summation of his military career. Most impressive was the fact that he had worked in so many third-world countries on humanitarian missions performing surgery on deformed youngsters. He repeated to us what he had previously told Tara: that little kids with diffuse axonal injuries can recover since their brains are pliable, whereas adults with such injuries have very little chance of recovery.

We took Shannon to PT. I supported Shannon's back and head so she could sit up as Jan did her hair. The PT ranged Shannon's feet. Under all this stimulation, Shannon did start to open her eyes peekaboo-style. Shannon fell into a deep sleep after the PT session. Her fever remained stable at 100 degrees. The hospital maintained the room temperature at a shivering 60 degrees.

Dr. FitzPatrick's nurse practitioner stopped by, stating he had called her from home with strict orders to check on Shannon. We told her Shannon seemed to be on a reverse cycle, more alert at nighttime and sleeping the bulk of the day. She told us that children in a coma can hear and we should keep talking to Shannon. Two speech therapists (STs) stopped by and saw that Shannon was in a deep sleep. That did not deter them as they recognized Phil Collins singing from the recent Disney movie *Tarzan*. They joined right in and belted out the chorus. I was glad Shannon had missed the brutal rendition.

My aunt who was a nun with the Immaculate Heart of Mary Order visited with a few other sisters, and they prayed over Shannon. They had their local and national convent leading the prayer campaign.

We all sat down as the weekend pediatric resident physician stopped by and checked Shannon. As the other doctors had, he went on and on about the long recovery process from brain injury. He put his tongue depressor stick in Shannon's mouth and tried to remove it. Shannon tightly clenched her teeth and would not let go. The doctor tried pulling it out from all different angles without success. Ten minutes later Nurse Mary returned and told the doctor to pull hard as she tickled Shannon's chin. The doctor went flying across the room as he extracted the tongue depressor. He held it up like a trophy and excused himself. The weekend resident physician had shared with us another dose of pessimism and then lost a battle for his tongue depressor with a three-year-old girl in a coma. I chose to believe that Shannon was sending a message that she knew of the prayers and would do all she could to let God answer them through her.

A gastroenterologist stopped by, and he was right off the set of a British comedy special. He was a six-foot-tall Chinese guy with a heavy British accent. He explained that he would have tests done and schedule the surgical procedure to place a feeding tube in Shannon's stomach. He was not giving us much choice and going on about how the tube would enable her to get more nutrition, which she needed to get stronger. Once the tube went in, it would stay for at least three months. We had hoped Shannon would be eating regularly much sooner than that.

Early in the afternoon, Shannon woke from her deep sleep but was still firmly in her coma. Her movement was much greater as she seemed to be trying to get comfortable in the bed amid the burden of three casts. It was amazing how we could differentiate between her waking and sleeping periods when she was in fact always unresponsive. I put her in the wheelchair and took her for a walk. My dad was visiting and looked devastated to see one of his eighteen grandchildren in a wheelchair. I reminded him it was just temporary.

My supervisor from US Customs and his wife were next to visit. I gave him a message to post on the electronic bulletin board that updated everyone on Shannon's progress.

Tara relieved us, and we returned to the Ronald McDonald House of Delaware for a dinner of London broil. The meals at the house were a pleasant surprise, with a different organization volunteering every night to cook. Each group prepared several courses with lots of desserts. We met other families who were in as desperate straits as we were, with children facing organ transplants, heart surgery, and large doses of chemotherapy for advanced cancers. Jan was getting to know the other moms, as they outnumbered the dads and were more eager to talk.

We returned to the hospital that night, and I returned to the chapel for my daily breakdown. When I returned to Shannon's room, Barry and his wife were there with insurance papers for me to sign and nutritious snacks. I made a point to hide them from Ramsey. We told Barry about the resident's struggle with his tongue depressor, the Chinese GI doctor, and Shannon's continued brief eye openings. Soon we were all laughing very hard. Thanks, Shannon, for providing such great material. Shannon's blood pressure was down to 104 over 61, her best reading yet.

Another preaccident photo of Shannon with her cat

4

TARZAN TO THE RESCUE

As Jan and I were getting dressed for a Sunday of many visitors, I noticed each of us had lost ten to twenty pounds. The stress of the past thirteen days was responsible for that. We returned to the hospital, and Tara reported that Shannon had been moving all night in an agitated state, including a half hour of audible crying. We planned to stay later with Shannon that night and inquire about adjusting medication to help Shannon have more peaceful nights. We also noticed that Shannon would occasionally yawn like a healthy person.

Up to fifteen visitors came throughout the day. My sisters each brought something we had requested for Shannon, like firm pillows; long white socks; additional books, movies or music tapes; or parish bulletins reflecting Shannon at the top of the church prayer list. Only the rehab resident physician and nurse practitioner stopped by for medical purposes. Fewer physician visits meant Shannon was getting better. We did take Shannon to PT and OT sessions, which consisted of more of the same limb ranging with different therapists that covered weekend sessions for the patients who were most in need of therapeutic stretching.

Nurse Mary was doing her thing all day and was reluctant to depart when her shift ended. She rolled in a TV with a video cassette player attached. We started playing Disney tapes on the VCR, opting for the classics *Sleeping Beauty, Beauty and the Beast,* and *Tarzan. Tarzan* had come out about a year prior and was the first movie in a theater we'd taken Shannon to, and it remained one of her favorites. She loved the music and storyline of gorillas protecting baby Tarzan in the jungle. Phil Collins sang on the entire soundtrack.

One musical sequence describing Tarzan's adolescent years was on. It featured Tarzan and his friends the young ape and elephant running through the jungle enjoying small tree limbs, refreshing ponds, and thin vegetation. ***Shannon opened both her eyes.*** First her right eye, two-thirds of the way, and then her left eye one-third of the way. She held both eyes open for fifteen seconds, closed them, and then reopened them for a longer time. She looked at us, at the TV, and back to us as if to suggest *Tarzan* deserved our attention.

Jan, Tara, and I all teared up and welcomed her back. She had a slight grin as she remained still instead of thrashing her arms. We looked up, and the room was full of nurses as overjoyed as we were. They dragged a young female resident physician in, stating she needed some good news. We had not met this physician before, but she was very young and Hispanic, and she looked like she had been working around the clock. Treating such severely ill children had to take its toll. Ramsey came over wearing a new Western outfit to share the excitement. A line formed out the door with respiratory therapists, maintenance employees, and parents of other patients. All wanted to share the good news, something that was always welcome in a rehab ward.

We stayed with her until midnight, when Shannon drifted into a deep sleep. We felt such relief and gratitude that Shannon had awoken from the coma and seemed to recognize us. She had not spoken any words but seemed more comfortable being awake, with less agitated movement.

Very smart and experienced doctors had said Shannon may not wake up for weeks to months. She woke up thirteen days and nine hours after being struck. Thanks to all physicians and nurses at Cooper and DuPont, especially Dr. Murza, Nurse Pat, and Nurse Mary. Thanks to my family, friends, and coworkers who had supported us and helped Shannon, especially Anne, with her medical expertise. We left the hospital exhilarated that Shannon's coma was over and committed to the long journey of recovery we had already undertaken.

On Monday morning I let Jan sleep in and returned to the hospital at 8:00 a.m. Tara said Shannon had had her best night yet. The new medication had helped her sleep. Shannon was currently awake and watching *Tarzan* again with her guardian angel, Nurse Mary. After the movie was over, I read her five books. Shannon looked around the room as Mary gave her a bath. She maintained eye contact with me and seemed to take comfort in my presence, as indicated by frequent smiles. Shannon's blood pressure and temperature had been stable for thirty-six hours. Mary told me to bring in Shannon's clothes and pajamas. I was like, "Whatever you say, angel. You and your TV acquisition basically woke Shannon up."

The parade of visiting doctors, nurses, and technicians started early, and all were overjoyed to see Shannon awake. They mentioned adjusting medicines to help her focus and trying something called Botox to help her limbs relax. They also scheduled a test for the next day to see if Shannon's swallowing reflex was intact. Their demeanor was much more upbeat than it had been last week.

Shannon's therapists were able to accomplish more with Shannon being alert. They took off one leg cast and worked on that limb for two hours. The ST said she finally had good things to write in her report.

I spent the day talking to and reading to Shannon. Seeing her awake gave us a surge of energy. Jan notified family and friends, including the PICU staff at Cooper Trauma Center, of her improvement. Shannon seemed to have had enough of *Tarzan*, so we switched to *Beauty and the Beast*. Two of my sisters visited with new outfits for Shannon and were delighted to find her awake.

We joined Shannon for her first PT session. Monica showed us how to stretch Shannon's feet by pushing the ball of the foot back and pulling down on the heel simultaneously, then holding for thirty seconds. Shannon's feet and hands still flexed inward. The next step was to have the orthopedic staff make thin, flexible braces that provided maximum support to her feet. The braces were called dynamic ankle foot orthoses, or DAFOs for short. They had to be a big improvement from the casts.

The rehab director, Dr. Ray, stopped by and asked us to consider a new treatment of injecting Shannon's feet with Botox. Botox was not approved by the FDA yet and was not commonly used. A few years later Botox became common for cosmetic purposes. I made a point to talk to Anne and get back to him.

Monica the PT had Shannon reacting to lights and sounds from different directions. She pushed a large gym ball to Shannon and told her to push it back. After a ten-second delay, Shannon complied with her request. Monica said that Shannon would need time to receive, understand, and respond to any request to do things. The two STs had a productive session with Shannon as they were overjoyed she was alert and responsive to sounds.

Shannon seemed worn out after the therapy session and promptly took a nap. The rehab attending physician updated us on several areas. Shannon's blood pressure was now stable, and there was no need to go with the patch to deliver medicine. Her blood was clotting more quickly now, and they considered giving her aspirin to slow it down. A test would take place tomorrow to see if she was able to chew and digest food. The surgical procedure to put a feeding tube in Shannon's stomach so she could get more nutrition was being scheduled for next week. Shannon needed to be weaned off Dilantin, as she was not having seizures, and prescribed a milder antiseizure medicine. Protocols required staying on such medication for an extended period following a traumatic brain injury. Ritalin would be prescribed now that Shannon was awake to help her focus. The dose of Tylenol every four hours would continue to help control fevers. Additional medicine would be maintained to help her sleep at night to keep her digestive tract working properly. Results of a recent CAT scan were forthcoming. The recent ultrasound of Shannon's stomach showed all organs intact. Shannon needed to be evaluated by the neurological ophthalmologist.

It was getting hard to remember all these details. I told myself to write things down and had a work friend drop off notebooks. It had been two weeks now of little sleep and the daily emotional roller coaster, and we were feeling the strain. I needed a plan to deal with the challenges.

Dr. FitzPatrick stopped by with a big smile and relaxed demeanor. He reported the CAT scan showed no additional bleeding and no further damage following the first scans at Cooper. He said the reduction of spasticity in Shannon's limbs and reduced fevers were signs that her brain was healing. He spoke to Shannon directly, asking her to stick out her tongue. Shannon responded with a raspberry, and everyone laughed. Dr. FitzPatrick said we were in great hands with Dr. Ray and his team and he looked forward to continued progress. We got the impression he was saying farewell as he had lots of critical patients requiring surgery, and that was fine.

Each day we got to know more kids facing life-threatening illnesses and their parents, who were struggling to maintain hope despite enormous odds. Several infants had successful organ transplants only to get an infection that could not be treated. They risked organ rejection, so no good options remained. The kids with cerebral palsy faced annual surgeries.

The hospital social worker spoke to us every other day. She was impressed by the amount of insurance we had and the volume of support our family was providing. She inquired about how we were feeling and suggested we attend weekly sessions with her to help us deal with the life-changing circumstances.

We were already getting some solid support from the Ronald McDonald House of Delaware family advocate named Marge. All the visitors and phone calls were great, but we were tired of answering questions, especially when our situation was so grim. The staff at the Ronald McDonald House knew to ask, "How did things go today?" as opposed to "What are the doctors telling you?" That gave us a chance to reply with Shannon's daily small victories, such as breathing on her own, sitting up, or tracking objects.

The Delaware State Police had scheduled a big display outside the hospital with all of their high-speed equipment. Unfortunately it rained, and the event was moved inside, which limited the number of items on exhibit. We took Shannon to the hospital's third floor and showed her some equipment. Shannon wanted no part of the bright lights or officers eager to demonstrate. She grew restless in her wheelchair and turned her head away from the policemen and equipment. After a few minutes, we left with the state troopers wishing us luck. The policemen gave up-close presentations of water rescue equipment and assault gear. Some kids observed from wheelchairs and some from stretchers. Touching or holding the ropes, shields, and lights seemed to make them feel better or at least take their minds off their severe illnesses. I wondered if I could ever show them such specialized features of my law enforcement agency, such as the canine teams in action.

The next few nights were still a struggle, with Shannon agitated at least half the time and very restless. Shannon had some productive OT and PT sessions in which she displayed better head control and some strength in the kneeling position when supported by our hands. We had decided to go with the Botox after Anne had informed us that it was on the verge of FDA approval and becoming common in the treatment of brain-injured kids.

Dr. Ray's assistant removed Shannon's leg casts. Dr. Ray came in his motorized wheelchair (he had had polio as a child) with two gigantic syringes and longer needles. He had actually been a patient at DuPont as a child and now ran the rehab division with great success. Shannon seemed to know the injection was for her. We held her tightly as Dr. Ray administered the large dose of Botox into her calves. Shannon winced in pain. I carried her back to her room, where Dr. FitzPatrick visited, once again, and commented on Shannon having more control over her tongue, another sign of improvement. Shannon looked good without her legs cast.

My brother Barry arrived and saw Shannon awake for the first time since his daily visits at Cooper. He was overjoyed and gave her a big hug. Shannon smiled at him but was not yet able to speak. I updated him on her awakening just prior to the two-week mark. We got to talking about work, and Barry said the only sick leave he had taken in the past twenty years had been three days for knee surgery. I was glad he was the lawyer on Shannon's case.

My parents and youngest sister, Kate, visited, and they saw Shannon awake for the first time since the accident. My mom was a very impressive woman, having raised ten kids, nine with college educations, and all having gone into admirable professions. My sister Kate had Down syndrome and required lots of special attention. My mom never complained. She just drove on and put the needs of her family first. Her upbeat attitude was most impressive. My parents' efforts at raising children clearly paid off as in this crisis, I was getting professional support in legal and medical fields from Barry and Anne and emotional and logistical support from the rest of the family. The twin sisters were both in early childhood education, and I planned on reaching out for their expertise when Shannon transitioned to the local school system. I felt for the families dealing with similar circumstances without big families to lean on for support. Shannon started a series of powerful yawns, which was wonderful to see as the breathing tube was gone. She drifted off to sleep looking very close to healthy with only one cast. The plan was to recast her feet after forty-eight hours of the Botox working.

My brother-in-law Greg gave Jan and me a ride back to our house.

We grabbed more clothes, videos, toys, and mail; checked phone messages; and drove our car back to the hospital. Shannon was awake and happy to see us. She was not talking but had lots of facial expressions and let out an audible laugh.

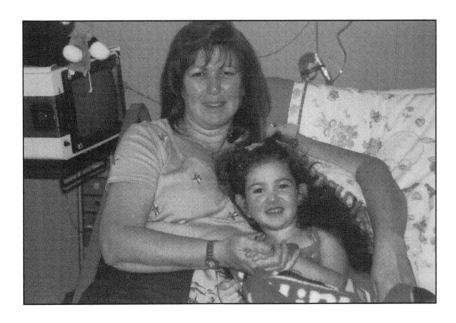

Shannon and Mom so happy to be together awake and alert with no medical apparatus in the way

5

TEAM SHANNON TAKES CHARGE

Dr. Ray's rehab unit had an organized approach that not even the US Military could match. He started weekly meetings with all professionals caring for Shannon. Nurse Mary had lots to say, and the PT, OT, and ST all had both shared and individual goals. The administrative person was present to get the facts needed by the insurance company. A neurological psychologist joined the team with plans to conduct regular sessions with Shannon focusing on her cognitive abilities. An education specialist also started sessions with her. Various resident or attending physicians would also join the meetings. Each meeting featured at least ten professionals all working together to develop and administer the best program for Shannon. Dr. Ray would seek input, then give direction, whether it was a medical topic, a procedural issue with the administration, or a short-term goal that everyone should focus on. With such a juggernaut assembled to work with Shannon, I decided it was time to return to work.

My inner circle, made up of my dad; my brother Barry, the attorney; several sisters; and a few friends had suggested I return to work and plan to take time off down the road when we brought Shannon home. They knew

I was the type that needed to stay busy to stay calm. I had used over three weeks of leave and had plenty remaining, but work could be a healthy outlet for the daily demons I struggled with. Fear for Shannon's struggles now and in the future and thoughts of guilt surfaced frequently. I requested a p.m. shift with my organization, which would enable me to be with Shannon in the mornings, then work eight hours, then return to DuPont and Ronald McDonald House of Delaware at night.

My first shift back was something else, as all gave me powerful hugs and shared positive thoughts and prayers. Some asked annoying questions such as "Is she walking and talking yet?" or "What are doctors telling you?" or shared their medical knowledge. Expectations of walking and talking were unreasonable and illustrated how long we still had to go. Few people know the severity of traumatic brain injuries and the marathon the recovery process is. I felt like I had to give them a briefing on brain injuries but lacked the energy to do this. Many commented on how much weight I had lost. I chose to focus on the positive and described all the things Shannon was doing and how far she had come. My mind was certainly with Shannon, and my focus was weak, but I managed to be productive given my ample experience. Shannon still had bouts with agitation the girls had to deal with. Who knew how long my insurance would last, so I needed to maintain income. I recorded myself reading books and talking to Shannon, hoping it could help calm her when I was not there.

All work environments are full of employees that complain and some that seek drama. US Customs is no different. The job requires a probing interaction with passengers to determine if they are legitimate businessmen or tourists. This makes for irate passengers who loudly voice their objections. Such complaints had no impact on me, as I was worried about bigger things. Coworkers sought agreement on their scheduling beef with management or other minor issues they made into mountains. A month ago I may have given them some feedback. Now I just plowed through and dreamed up new material for Shannon's workouts. Amazing how your perspective can change so drastically in a short time.

Commuting back and forth from DuPont to work gave me more alone time, and the tears just flowed on nearly every trip. Better to let it out than hold the stress in. I returned one night to the hospital, and Shannon was not in her room. The same spine-tingling sensations I had had in the first days after the accident returned with force. Where could she be? Back in intensive care for some kind of surprise infection? I wanted to yell and get the entire night staff on the search but stayed calm as I walked toward the nurses' station. The station was empty, but it was close to the conference room. That's where I found Shannon. Jan had moved her bed since Shannon's agitated roommate was sounding off very loudly. What waves of relief! It was not uncommon to hear kids screaming at night as they dealt with nightmares, seizures, or various neurological disorders. The proficient nurses promptly responded to tweak medication or provide comfort. I made a note to talk to Dr. Ray, as Shannon needed rest to recover.

Over the next few days, Shannon showed continued improvement and participated fully in most therapy sessions. She smiled and laughed for therapists, and it didn't take long for them to be hooked on her. Monica the PT was impressed with the Botox results, and Shannon's feet being nimbler. After her therapy sessions, Shannon was showing real interest in her favorite Disney movies. She paid close attention to *Cinderella* and loved the parts where the princess was caring for the animals and the small animals were jousting for accommodations.

Shannon did well on the study to determine if she could safely chew and swallow baby food. She struggled on the water-swallowing test. She was able to start eating pureed food, which was a great improvement on the liquid nourishment the NG tube delivered. Nurse Mary was overjoyed with this and immediately contacted the dining staff to prepare her recommended dishes. We eagerly fed Shannon the pureed food, recalling from her first year what flavors of baby food she preferred. Apples and pears brought a real smile to her face. Providing such care to our child boosted our spirits as we had some control over her well-being.

Shannon started working with the teachers on staff on following orders and basic games. She responded with consistency, even though it took her up to twenty seconds to understand and respond to the request. For example, she was told to knock over the blocks in front of her. Shannon would hesitate for ten seconds, then start moving her arm to complete the act and finish after ten more seconds. I chose to focus on the accomplishment instead of the delay. Shannon was just about able to turn over in her PT sessions. The rehab gym was full of patients at times. One teenager was screaming his head off as therapists worked on his leg. Toddlers with hip replacements were required to stand to enable the hip to start doing its job, and they fought through the pain. We were able to participate in Shannon's workouts by pushing gym balls and basically playing with her.

Monica must have sensed our exhaustion one day as she stacked pillows high and got Shannon to toss them at us with assistance. She would grab the pillow with both hands, raise it high as Monica supported her trunk, and toss it a few feet at Jan and me. I reacted like they were the most powerful shots in the world and hit the floor with rolls and lots of noise. Shannon started to laugh uncontrollably and continued the onslaught with more tosses. I crawled back so they would strike me, causing further injury. A visiting PT was carrying a video recorder looking for positive results in sessions for a graduate-degree program. She asked us for permission to film Shannon and even had a form to fill out. We continued the pillow drill and were overjoyed at Shannon's enthusiastic response.

Shannon was achieving goals at a rapid pace. The rehab staff set a target discharge date of September 15, which was seven weeks away. They also scheduled a gastrointestinal tube to be surgically placed in her stomach. This would enable her to get more nutrition since her slow-paced eating of pureed food was not providing enough. This reinforced just how complex a situation we were in. The last few days' progress had been great, but Shannon had a long way to go.

Monica the PT started using a "stander" in which Shannon was strapped to a board that rotated to a vertical position. This enabled more blood flow to her legs. Monica also made head control a priority. Shannon soon could turn her head when called and visually track us when we walked around. I continued strenuous efforts to comfort Shannon when she got agitated with somersaults and cartwheel attempts, which Shannon and others in the gym laughed at. The neurological ophthalmologist finally got her chance to check Shannon and gave us good news of no structural damage to Shannon's eyes. She said that Shannon demonstrated difficulty in finding things and had limited peripheral vision, especially on the left side. She would talk to the OT about activities to help Shannon's vision.

Shannon's routine was set with intense PT sessions that stretched her muscles. The OT sessions were challenging but entertaining, full of cognitive activities such as pressing buttons to get light responses and responding to all sorts of stimuli. Shannon celebrated at lunch by eating her pureed food while watching Disney movies. *Pinocchio* and *The Lion King* were the latest classics that she watched and enjoyed. She took a nap after lunch and attended ST in the afternoon. Three days a week, she went to the education specialists for more stimulating activities.

Shannon's agitation did return several times a day and lasted at least an hour. She must have been frustrated with recognizing how restricted she was as compared to her healthy self. I would stay with her for morning therapy sessions, then go to work and get back around 10:00 p.m. I had drafted a letter of Shannon's progress and gave it to people when they asked. I was grateful for their support but very tired of answering questions.

On a stop at home, I put the letters in neighbors' mailboxes, which were all decorated with yellow ribbons in support of Shannon. The same large ribbon decorated each mailbox at every house on the street. This represented a coordinated effort among the neighbors to send the message all were hoping and praying for Shannon. What a feeling to make the right turn on our street and see a gigantic yellow ribbon on every mailbox.

I envisioned escorting Shannon with a scissor someday, hopefully soon, as she cut the ribbons and thanked the neighbors for the support. The weekend brought lots of visitors, and all were thrilled with Shannon's progress, including many of Shannon's young cousins who were seeing her for the first time post injury.

Nurse Mary was busy knocking out one team goal after the next. She got Shannon to use the toilet on a regular basis—with support, of course. She taught Shannon to greet her therapists with waves and smiles. Mary had a habit of folding her arms or placing them at her sides when she was trying to make a point. Shannon remarkably started to imitate her. What a connection they had. For the next week, we constantly heard the entire staff ask Shannon to imitate Nurse Mary. This was a clear example of Shannon following commands, which was another goal.

The weekly meeting was full of goals accomplished, replaced by new, more challenging goals of holding her head up for five minutes, sitting up with arms down, and following commands with more consistency. The GI tube placement was scheduled for the next day. We were not happy with this but decided to trust the experts. We also were disappointed to find out Shannon was to stay on antiseizure medicine for an entire year. Dr. Ray stated it was time to get moving on Shannon's feet, which had been recently recast. He pushed his staff to coordinate with the department that made the orthopedic braces for the model that worked best for Shannon. Dr. Ray also said, "If you do not see Shannon for two days, you miss lots of improvements."

The following morning Shannon had a kick-ass PT session highlighted by thirty minutes in the stander with Monica dancing with her to popular kids' tunes like "The Hokey Pokey." At 1:30 p.m. Nurse Mary took her to the operating room for the GI tube insertion. Jan broke down as Shannon was away from us again in the hands of a full surgical team. Ten minutes later a tall doctor of Norwegian descent briefed us that all had gone well. We went to see Shannon in the recovery room and found her alert with the vital signs monitor reflecting healthy numbers across the board. What a change from the last time she was being monitored so closely. By 3:00 p.m. Shannon was back in her room laughing at *Pinocchio*.

Jan was dealing with the trauma of seeing Shannon struck by the vehicle and perhaps guilt, which I was also feeling. I made a point of getting her to discuss it with Marge of the Ronald McDonald House. There was also a neurological psychologist whom we had met briefly after arriving. We had not seen her since. She led a session and presented a plan to counsel us through dealing with our new realities. She was impressed that we had such an understanding of Shannon's injuries and told us it was contributing to the results we were seeing. I got the feeling her main message was that we should be prepared for peaks and valleys, especially when we transitioned to the school system, where cognitive deficits could be identified. We had enough to worry about now and hoped to put off crossing that bridge until we came to it.

Shannon's next PT session was tough, with Monica pushing her to sit up supported for thirty minutes with lots of ten-second periods of no support, then helping Shannon go from a sitting to standing position supported. Shannon worked hard and was able to accomplish this high standard with assistance. She was rewarded with peaches for lunch.

Shannon was sleeping better at night, with less agitation. I was able to concentrate at work and produce some fine seizures in the passenger and cargo environments. On one trip from work back to the hospital late at night, I got lost and ended up in Dover, Delaware. The grind must have been taking its toll. I told myself to power through. Stopping to rest could bring time to think, which I tried to avoid. The odds were against us in returning to normal family life. Being temporarily disoriented near the air force base in Dover on a dark, rainy night reminded me of the last time I had been so sleep deprived.

My army unit was tasked with conducting exercises in West Germany just a few kilometers from the East German Border during the last few years of the Cold War. On one such night, we had just returned from a training exercise in which rain, heavy fog, and fatigued soldiers made navigation a challenge and operation completion seemingly insurmountable. We managed to complete the exercise with all personnel safe, all equipment undamaged, and everyone eager for a few hours of sleep. If I could tap into that level of focus and endurance about ten years ago, I could dig deeper now and demonstrate the resilience needed to power through and help Shannon recover.

The next day I departed at 6:00 a.m. for a seventy-mile trip to Fort Dix, New Jersey, to run a shooting range for my military reserve unit. It was a brutally hot and sunny August day. The soldiers struggled to shoot well and qualify, but it felt good to have such missions to occupy my mind. I drove back that night and got a gigantic smile and hug from Shannon. While I was gone, she had mastered new tricks of sticking out her tongue on command and pointing to her nose or ears upon request.

I was worn out from the day spent on a rifle qualification range in the hot sun. Jan made me a large drink of ice, water, and grape juice from the nurses' station stash, which the nurses had welcomed us to use. I sat with Shannon and started to read her a book. I was very focused on this task but still noticed several patients' fathers stopping by to visit Shannon. It was more common to see them on weekends, as most worked during the week. Still, I wondered if they were hoping to admire Jan and Tara and their natural beauty as their glances at the girls grew a little too long. I was reluctant to voice the characters of the book I was reading to Shannon with the hospital neighbors close by.

I was accustomed to such staring as men commonly checked out my wife, looked at me briefly, then back at Jan, looking a bit surprised. Perhaps they were thinking, *How could a normal guy like him land a classy knockout like her?* Some would speak up: "Where did you guys meet?" We met at JFK Airport, where she worked for an airline and I worked for US Customs. Her arrival in the Customs Hall to help process passengers often stopped traffic as coworkers, skycaps, baggage handlers, and passengers all admired her appearance, class, and style. Weeks later all knew of our courtship and raised objections, wishing they had such luck at romance. Managers even sent me on more dangerous missions such as hospital duty with passengers who were internal drug smugglers or prisoner transport jobs with powerful offenders. Perhaps they hoped I would get injured and knocked out and thus would be unavailable to continue to be Jan's boyfriend.

JFK employees airport-wide approached her with flirtation and date requests. She politely refused all and focused on our relationship. I told some to cease fire on their efforts and suggested they may have better luck by approaching the hundreds of other female employees that worked for other airlines. No one became too confrontational, and the managers eased up on hazardous missions. We grew closer and fulfilled our plans of getting married and starting a family. But still, some level of gawking took place wherever we went.

Shannon's first session on Monday was with the teachers, and she cried her head off. For the first time, Nurse Mary had to be called into a session to calm her down. She recovered in time for a productive PT session highlighted by popping bubbles. I called Nurse Pat from Cooper that night and briefed her on all the new developments. She was in her glory and promised to call Jan soon to hear her version of the great news.

On Tuesday we took Shannon to the hospital dentist, who checked and cleaned her teeth. Shannon held her mouth open as if she did not have a brain injury. In PT Shannon played basketball as she shot a Nerf ball to a shorter rim with surprising accuracy. In OT Shannon stacked cups with precision while sitting up unsupported for over thirty minutes. Dr. Ray stopped by and suggested that a small amount of Botox in Shannon's left wrist may help with her grip. Shannon was comfortable with her therapists. We were able to talk to the social worker and neurological psychologist during her sessions.

That night we took Shannon to the Ronald McDonald House of Delaware for her first outing. The house was impressive, with walls full of uplifting artwork and flower arrangements on every table in the dining area. The staff scheduled various activities for the guests such as art for the kids, movie night, and pet-therapy night. On pet-therapy night, three gorgeous dogs visited with their handlers and performed tricks. The dogs then let the kids pet, hug, and squeeze them in a reckless way. Seeing the kids forget their illnesses for a few minutes was something else for the children and the parents. Shannon watched and sat on the floor petting one dog named Kirby, who was a small sheltie about three years old. She lasted an entire hour at the house before getting tired. We took her back to her room elated that the trip had gone so well.

The nursing staff tried to keep any noisy patients from sharing the room with Shannon. This led to a series of roommates staying for one night only for procedures like getting tonsils out. It was different talking to the parents who were sweating their twenty-four-hour hospital stay, especially when grandparents visited and went overboard in celebrating their grandchild's strength in enduring a routine procedure.

We started to take Shannon on walks throughout the hospital and met parents who had had over one hundred hospital visits with their chronically ill children. Jan liked to talk to the parents. All agreed that DuPont was a great facility. I was less vocal and usually adjourned to the chapel or parents' lounge to use the internet connection to look up details on traumatic brain injuries. Nearly all the data was negative.

Shannon was still not speaking but did have an audible laugh, cry, and sigh. She gave us magnificent smiles and hugs. She laughed appropriately at my antics, her Disney videos, and her therapist's games. Her agitation surfaced every few hours, and she was inconsolable, crying, shaking her head from side to side, and moving her limbs in a frustrated manner. It was as though she was frustrated with her ambulatory abilities having disappeared and aware her limbs were not complying with her brain's requests for stable movement.

Shannon had progressed with her chewing and swallowing process and was able to digest small pieces of fruit. She also could wave to visitors and play catch with them or present pages of a coloring book she had started to scribble in. She could promptly respond to simple commands such as stick out your tongue, close your eyes, and shake hands. We took her to the hospital activity center, which had a selection of new books and gigantic stuffed animals.

All of these improvements were a real relief, but the thoughts of where we had been a few weeks ago were still present. Dr. Ray's team saw an opportunity and seized it. It was time to push Shannon so her gross motor skills could be regained. The staff told us we were no longer welcome in her therapy sessions as Shannon would show separation anxiety and had to overcome it. We dropped her off in the therapy gym and saw a walker designed for small kids. We knew that Monica, Shannon's PT since day one in rehab, was on-site and ready to roll.

Jan went to the Ronald McDonald House and spoke to the staff and other moms. I decided to exercise and went to the hospital gym to shoot a few baskets or to the employee weight room. Some days I had good workouts, and other days the security guards chased me from the premises stating they were for "employees only." I hit the hospital library and did some brain injury research and found more grim prognoses and descriptions of long recoveries. When we picked up Shannon after therapy, she was glad to see us and usually demonstrated her latest accomplishment, such as standing by herself or taking a few steps with the walker.

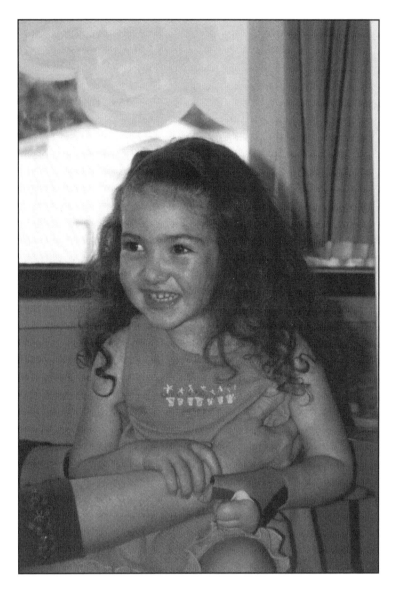

Shannon proud of herself showing how
she can sit up again with support

Shannon responds to the doctor's prompt to find her ears

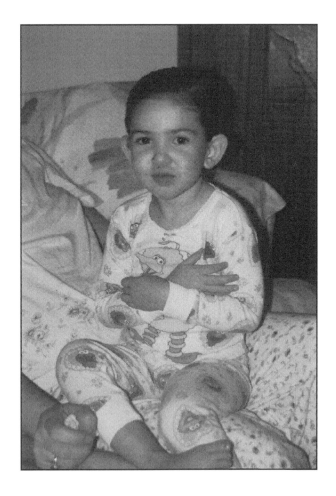

Shannon crossing her arms to imitate her favorite nurse

6

KIRBY PROVIDES A BREAKTHROUGH!

Shannon was clearly growing stronger and was able to sit and stand unsupported for longer periods of time. She was also more alert and aware of visitors, other patients, doctors, and nurses. Shannon expanded her Nurse Mary imitation to include facial expressions that went with the folded arms. The chemistry between them was remarkable. Mary would frequently whisper in Shannon's ear, which made her smile. Who knew what she was saying? Shannon had yet to speak, and we were getting worried. Her laughter and tears and occasional moans of frustration were audible. The doctors and therapists said they did not know when Shannon would speak.

We started taking Shannon to the Ronald McDonald House of Delaware on a regular basis. She was more engaged each time with remembering staff members and eager to see them or play with the vast array of toys. Her friend Kirby visited twice a week, and Shannon always perked up while watching his tricks or profusely petting him. We would have Shannon standing unsupported with one of us close by to catch her when she lost balance. The presence of Kirby enabled her to set new records by standing a few minutes. Kirby's handler commented on Shannon appearing stronger week after week. We agreed but said she was not speaking yet. The handler had a T-shirt with a picture of Kirby on it and told Shannon it was hers if Shannon could say Kirby's name. With no hesitation whatsoever, Shannon responded with enthusiasm, "*Ki-Ki-Kirby.*"

The handler gave Shannon the shirt as I broke down in tears of happiness. Staff members gathered to recognize this milestone as I tried to recompose myself. We put the shirt on Shannon as she posed with Kirby. Other parents congratulated us. Most of them needed such good news as they also had challenging medical ordeals. I found out the next day that Nurse Mary had been working with Shannon on forming words. Jan was allergic to dogs, and I was never a big fan since struggling with them on a paper-delivery route in the 1970s. I also had participated in training with army canine teams on my May stint at Fort Drum with the army. I was a role player and played the bad guy who got taken down by the dog. Arm sleeves prevented injury, but the clench of their jaws was still painful. That all changed as Kirby and his handler had achieved a remarkable vocal breakthrough with Shannon.

The next day we were in a session with the neurological psychologist that focused more on coping strategies for parents dealing with the realities of a brain-injured child. The doctor had a model house with figures for family members. Shannon picked up the mom figure and said, "Mom" as she handed it to Jan. This time Jan broke down in tears. Thirty minutes later Shannon got tired of the session and pointed to the door and said, "Go." Back in her room, we told Nurse Mary, and she celebrated with Shannon as they'd been working on the "Mom" utterance. That was what Mary had been occasionally whispering in Shannon's ear.

On our next trip to the Ronald McDonald House, which always had a large collection of pastry desserts, Shannon pointed to the latest and said, "Cake." In twenty-four hours Shannon had said "Kirby," "Mom," "go," and "cake." She seemed to be trying to say "hi" and "bye." The entire rehab floor staff increased the frequency of their visits, hoping to catch Shannon's new comments. The STs were the happiest as the work they were doing with facial exercises had paid off. They had recovered Shannon's voice and put it to work on relearning dozens of words and eventually phrases.

Shannon continued to grow stronger and make progress in her PT sessions. Monica had her riding a tricycle by herself all over the rehab gym and adjacent hallways. Shannon could turn over while lying down with ease and was working toward transitioning from lying down to sitting up by herself. Each day Shannon was taking a few more steps on her walker. Her feet were supported by new DAFOs, which provided lots of support but were thin enough that she could wear them in her shoes. They went up to her calves, almost to her knees. Many of the kids in the rehab ward had these braces. In their usual tone, the experts said Shannon would need such orthopedic support devices for the rest of her life.

I had started to spend occasional nights after work at our house, as we needed a game plan for when Shannon was discharged. Making the transition to outpatient would drastically cut the medical expenses and stretch the insurance policies for months of coverage for therapy sessions. The projected outpatient program was nearly identical to the inpatient one, with up to six hours a day of some form of therapy. Shannon was not yet strong enough to commute back and forth, so we planned to all stay at Ronald McDonald House of Delaware and come home on weekends.

After one trip home, I returned with Shannon's cat and reunited them at the Ronald McDonald House. Shannon was in her glory, and so was the cat. They spent a few hours getting reacquainted. It was clear Shannon remembered him, and we were glad to see she used the same tricks of dressing up her cat in clothes. I took a nap during this session and was surprised when my wife told me I had been out for four hours. I was starting to feel constantly tired but knew I had to drive on. I remembered comments another army officer in my unit made when some of us expressed frustration at the pace of field exercises and prime years in our early twenties spent in the German countryside on maneuver exercises. Most thought we were wasting our time, but this guy said we would not know for years whether it was worth it or not. It turned out it was worth it for me as I knew I could drive on for weeks at a frantic pace on little sleep since I had done it with the Eleventh Armored Cavalry Regiment.

Shannon had an amazing PT session with Monica, highlighted by taking fourteen unsupported steps to balloons. She also showed progress playing catch and handling a paintbrush. She made a flawless transition to ST by getting a perfect score on picking the right objects. OT was next. Shannon got agitated and did not cooperate with the therapist. Dr. Ray was frequently around in his motorized wheelchair watching such progress. At our weekly meeting, he said Shannon was ready to be discharged as an inpatient. *Yes!*

*Shannon and Kirby together posing in
celebration of their joint effort to regain her speaking skills*

7

TRANSITION HOME TURNS INTO

A ROLLER COASTER

I was starting to feel the impact of eight weeks of the grind from this life-changing event. I was usually late to work after spending all morning and early afternoon with Shannon and found myself yawning nonstop. Jan and Tara were also wearing down, as they were arguing over Shannon's outfits, hairstyles, and the nurse rotation. Some of the fill-in nurses, beyond Nurse Mary and Heather, the overnight nurse, were not as familiar with Shannon as those two were. We found ourselves arguing over what techniques we should employ to deal with Shannon's agitation. All the comments the experts made about us hitting a wall seemed accurate. Family and friends continued to visit. Those who had not seen her since Cooper were amazed at the transformation. Their exhilaration at the progress gave us the strength to drive on.

I had been working with the hospital administration and social workers to pay for Shannon's treatment. While we had good coverage through auto and health policies, it could not last forever. Shannon's stay at Cooper was all in intensive care and very expensive. DuPont's costs were more manageable, but we had run through half of our auto policy and a big chunk of our health policy. Getting Shannon discharged to outpatient status would extend our resources greatly, so that became our main goal.

Shannon continued to make significant progress. We picked her up after OT one day and were shocked to find her using scissors to cut shapes from paper. She held the paper with one hand and manipulated the scissors safely with the other hand. We did not expect such fine dexterity so soon. Monica the PT created an amazing climax to the PT sessions of Shannon walking to us with her walker from across the rehab gym.

Such success was interspersed with bouts of agitation. We were not present for those sessions but struggled to comfort Shannon after her frustration peaked. We had taken her all over the hospital, hoping the movement and new sites would provide some comfort. We ran into some of the PICU nurses, respiratory techs, and x-ray techs, and they could not believe Shannon's progress. They suggested we visit the PICU, and I made a point to follow through on that suggestion as PICU doctors and nurses do not see a lot of positive results. Few kids return to share their progress.

Shannon seemed to remember the other kids on the rehab floor. A toddler named Dan had a party to celebrate his discharge, and Shannon was happy to attend. Infants were in other rooms, and Shannon suggested frequent visits by pointing at the rooms and saying, "Baby." On one occasion I was trying to get Shannon to sleep after three grueling hours of therapy, and a young boy burst into the room and collapsed. His mom was right behind him apologizing and yelling for the nurse to report her son's unexpected seizure. Shannon was alarmed at the intrusion. She tried to tell her mom of this by pointing at the door and struggling to say, "Boy."

The floor was busier than ever as kids with cerebral palsy needed surgical procedures and subsequent therapy for their arms and legs, which had such spasticity. Late-summer activities brought more victims of near-drownings or car accidents. Other parents started reaching out to us frequently about how Shannon was making such amazing progress. Jan was very willing to discuss things with them at length with all the credit going to nurses and therapists. I was still the quiet one and lacked the energy to give much of a reply.

All were content with the plan to discharge Shannon in a few days for Labor Day weekend. Nurse Mary gave us a class on administering medication to Shannon through her G-tube. Shannon was down to three types of medication. One was to prevent seizures, another to stimulate her cognitively, and a third to help with digestion. Monica let us participate in Shannon's last PT session as an inpatient. Shannon now had some core strength to hurl balls, pillows, and the like and made PT an entertaining workout. She got to run mini obstacle courses and was rewarded by riding on my back. My antics made Shannon laugh so hard she got hiccups. In OT Shannon could stand by herself for brief periods and reach up and paint on a board. Shannon was now eating lots of soft food, such as mashed potatoes, grilled cheese, pizza, and small pieces of oranges and bananas. She was still getting bolus nourishment through her G-tube at nighttime, but as soon as we went home, that was not required as long as she ate well.

I made a run home with all of the material Shannon had accumulated over the last two months, such as Vermont Teddy Bears, stuffed animals, Barbie dolls, and new books. I told the neighbors she would be back on Friday but that we did not want any festivities other than a brief visit to avoid overstimulation and possible agitation. I reconnoitered the best routes back to DuPont with the least number of hills and turns as Nurse Mary warned us the antiseizure medication would cause motion sickness. I booked a room in the Ronald McDonald House of Delaware for each Monday through Thursday in September with us returning home on the weekends. All was set for Shannon to be discharged. I had phone numbers for Nurse Mary, Nurse Heather, and the rehab unit attending physician and would call them if necessary. The past seven weeks at DuPont had been grueling, but we had the miracle we had hoped and prayed for and were confident Shannon would continue to make progress.

We packed up the car and set off for home. Traffic was brutal on the Friday of Labor Day weekend. I had not anticipated this and could do nothing but wait. The cars were packed up and headed to the Jersey Shore for the last summer excursion for all. Some cars had bicycles strapped to the trunks for use on boardwalks. Others had fishing poles for beach use.

We were focused on administering Shannon's medicine without the nurses and hoping she did OK with returning to her house and seeing neighbors. Many cars would cut off each other to save a few seconds of travel time. I welcomed the slow pace. Perhaps it was keeping Shannon's motion sickness at bay. I thought of the irony of parents rushing to spend time with their kids. None of them had spent more time with their kids than we had with Shannon over the last two months. Certain moments were painful, harrowing, and very difficult, but we got through them and were still a family going to celebrate Labor Day weekend. Dare I say it was time well spent?

Shannon did OK with the ride, vomiting only twice as opposed to the five times we expected. She was very delighted to get home, with lots of smiles and waving to neighbors and laughing at one two-year-old who had lost his bathing suit. She went right to her playroom and rejoiced in her familiar toys and the comfort of home. One of her favorite preaccident toys was a small bird figure that would chirp when you balanced it in the right way on your finger under the bird's chin. She picked it up, remembered the technique, and had the bird singing aloud. This took real memory, several brain systems working together, and attention to detail. Jan and I hugged Shannon and each other in relief. I could not wait to share this with Team Shannon on Monday. We got her to sleep at eleven and crashed ourselves without even unloading the car.

We let Shannon sleep in her own bed as she had had no issues preaccident. We did use the common rails to prevent her from falling out of the bed. I crashed on the floor beside her to make sure she slept fine. I checked on her every hour. Around 3:00 a.m. I noticed her cat was in her bed curled up around her feet. He was happy she had returned, so I let him stay there, knowing he would ease any agitation when Shannon woke up. This was the first night Shannon had been in her own bed in two months without a nurse nearby and one of us awake monitoring all. It was great to see her transition back smoothly.

We got up early on Saturday and made Shannon her first post accident breakfast at home. It consisted of small pieces of apples, toast, and some red juice she liked. Shannon vomited the red juice, which was no surprise as it was the first time in months she had had it. Our first activity was washing the car with Shannon handling the hose from her wheelchair. Shannon acknowledged neighbors that visited with smiles and demonstrations of how to use the hose. She fired the hose back and forth from the car to me and laughed at the results. I was soaking wet but in my glory, as Shannon was home enjoying a routine activity.

Shannon's friend Brian from next door visited, and she greeted him by taking an amazing twenty-seven steps unsupported to the playroom, where they played catch and stacked blocks. Shannon needed and took a long nap. Brian waited on her to wake up and took her for a ride around the block in his wagon, which was a better model than the hospital version, with high sides that provided real support. I only had to watch and hold Shannon's hand at times over the bumpy stretches of sidewalk. They continued to play in the backyard, but Shannon got restless, and we had to give her Tylenol. They returned to the playroom, and Shannon shared some OT knowledge by getting Brian to join her in cutting baseball figures (more challenging than cutting straight lines), coloring, and tossing balls. Another of Shannon's preaccident activities was attaching ropes to chairs by making knots that her cat could not resist. We were encouraged when she resumed this process. The ropes were loose and the knots weak, but she remembered the concept. It was great to be home and encouraging to see Shannon recall some favorite toys and preaccident routines.

The next day brought more activities, with Shannon showing real agitation. It was like she recognized she could not run around the house like before and could not communicate well. She insisted on being carried almost all day. Her Disney videos did not help much as Shannon would repeatedly ask to be carried upstairs and five minutes later ask to be carried downstairs.

Shannon demonstrating unforgotten skills on her first trip home. She balanced this bird on her finger, resulting in the bird singing. She remembered the trick, which both Jan and I celebrated enthusiastically.

8

RONALD MCDONALD HOUSE OF
DELAWARE PROVIDES LAYERS OF RELIEF

On our return to DuPont Monday, Shannon fell asleep in the car, which obviated the motion sickness. She was still cranky and did not do much in her PT and OT sessions but did crawl around the gym at a faster rate. After a day of therapy sessions, we returned to the Ronald McDonald House of Delaware with Shannon with us instead of in her hospital room, which was great. I finally had a few minutes to learn the history of Ronald Mcdonald House Charities (RMHC).

The first Ronald McDonald House was opened in 1974 thanks to the support of a community of people in Philadelphia. Recognizing the need to provide a place to stay and meals for families of children being treated at hospitals, members of the community worked together to raise the funds to open the first Ronald McDonald House and begin the mission of RMHC. Since local McDonald's restaurants were involved with fundraising, the House was named after McDonald's iconic mascot, Ronald McDonald, since he represents joy and happiness, something families can use when they have an ill or injured child. Today the global charity has over 375 house programs in 62 countries and regions, as well as 260-plus Ronald McDonald Family Room programs in hospitals and 40-plus Ronald McDonald Care Mobile programs that bring medical and dental services to underserved communities around the world.

The house we stayed in for several months in Wilmington, Delaware, was run by a handful of full-time employees and hundreds of volunteers. One group of volunteers provided meals, another provided fresh flowers throughout the house, another provided cookies and pastries, another provided landscaping services, another provided therapy dogs to work with the ill kids and their siblings, and another provided transportation. I did not know it yet, but we were about to benefit greatly from all services.

We had real time on our hands for the first time in two months, and the Ronald McDonald House of Delaware had the resources to help our family in countless ways. It had a gigantic playroom with big and small toys; a library with thousands of kids' books; nightly activities like pet therapy, arts, and crafts; Disney movies and popular kids TV shows; and grounds with patios, gazebos, and gardens that were very well maintained. Just looking at the walls covered with uplifting images of blue skies, white clouds, and bright suns provided more visual stimulation for Shannon. Each table in the kitchen had a fresh bouquet of flowers. A different volunteer group cooked a full-course dinner each night. The desserts were my favorite as another volunteer group made an impressive selection and volume of cookies every few days.

The staff had all gotten to know Shannon and looked forward to hearing nightly reports of her daily victories. A nice married couple visited every Sunday and gave massages to parents. They did not like it when I showed up, as both commented my torso was among the tightest they had ever stroked. That was during our first few weeks at the house. Shannon's progress was gradually loosening me up. Jan had gotten to know several families, and the women loved to discuss the course of their hospitalized kids' treatments. It seemed almost every night classic piano tunes would be heard as a parent would start playing to vent from medical realities.

After dinner I would take Shannon for walks around the house and adjacent grounds in her stroller. My pockets were lined with chocolate-chip and oatmeal cookies for dessert and snacks for the critters. We would look for squirrels, rabbits, or the occasional possum. Upon locating one, Shannon would point and say, "Go." I would push the stroller in a short sprint, and the critters would run up trees or down holes. As we waited on their return, I would eat the cookies and demonstrate how to wind up and throw. Shannon would toss leftover cookies to entice them back. Shannon loved this game and laughed hard when we succeeded in finding and feeding the wildlife. She laughed harder when the possums went underground. Upon our return, Shannon would mumble and laugh to her Mom about our adventures. She would point outside and mumble sounds similar to "cookie" and "squirrel." Within a week the cookie supply was depleted, but the volunteers delivered a larger batch. They wondered who was eating so many cookies.

Shannon now saw her friend Kirby the sheltie twice a week and would take him for a walk with no hesitation whatsoever. The walk was down the hallway and back, a journey Shannon made proudly with her head up and leaning on Kirby for support the entire trip. It seemed that Shannon was able to entertain Kirby more at every visit. She was sitting longer and walking farther. Kirby had his own following of new and old friends. A few other dogs also participated. They mainly got hugs from the kids and followed basic commands of sitting, presenting paws, and turning around, and the kids rewarded them with treats. Kirby was the top dog with his jumping in and out of hoops, rolling all over the floor, and being so responsive to unhealthy kids. Kirby's handler, Lisa, and her husband, Dan, seemed to be getting as much satisfaction as the families. Dan was busy snapping pictures, which were posted on the walls. Kirby also visited Shannon in the hospital as the rehab wing had days and times when the dogs would visit the kids in their rooms. Pet therapy was a new field, with the dogs getting real results. If it had not been for Kirby and the other dogs, Shannon would have become agitated more frequently, and we had seen enough of that.

The other families were facing daunting medical challenges of their own. One young man was there with his grandmother from Puerto Rico waiting on an urgent kidney transplant. Another teenager had a disease that caused weak bones and had broken bones over fifty times. Several parents were donating one of their kidneys to their infant in need. Other families had scary cancer diagnoses and were veterans of DuPont visits and Ronald McDonald House stays as their kids faced radiation, chemotherapy, and bone-marrow transplants. There must have been five countries and fifteen states represented, as DuPont Hospital had a national reputation in brain injury treatment and organ transplants. Other kids had conditions that severely limited their growth and made their bones brittle.

We welcomed a family we had met at Cooper Trauma Center. Their twelve-year-old son had lost his leg in a quad vehicle accident. They were very happy to see friendly, familiar faces at the hospital and the Ronald McDonald House of Delaware. They were amazed at Shannon's progress and were confident their son could do well. The house had age-appropriate activities for their son—movies and video games.

The staff and volunteers of our house did a great job keeping the place clean as these kids were at high risk for infection. I promised myself that once Shannon had regained her health, I would become an advocate for the house and repay this enormous debt. Our house was great for keeping families together and taking care of their basic needs so they could focus on their sick child. In one of my brain injury research sessions in the hospital library, I saw a harrowing statistic that in families where there is a traumatic brain injury, the divorce rate is 90 percent, and the bankruptcy rate is 95 percent. I was counting on the Ronald McDonald House of Delaware to help keep my family together.

One young man from Iowa was facing an aggressive form of cancer. The disease or the radiation and chemotherapy had turned his skin to unhealthy colors and made him very bloated. He had a wheelchair that he powered with his chin, as his limbs had no strength. He still had a big smile and managed to enjoy his time at the Ronald McDonald House of Delaware. I got to know his dad as we discussed farming in Iowa and the difficulty of bringing his son from Iowa to DuPont in a ground ambulance.

Another five-year-old boy we knew from the rehab wing had gone in the swimming pool after his pet and saved the dog but nearly drowned himself. His mom had found him and called an ambulance; the EMTs had performed CPR to save him. The lack of oxygen before they arrived resulted in motor and cognitive impairments. He was one of the kids whose dad never visited the hospital. The mom was on a solo mission, and she chose to commute most days from forty miles away instead of taking advantage of the Ronald McDonald House of Delaware. We tried to convince her to stay at the house, which was right next to the hospital, but did not succeed. Perhaps she commuted home to spend time with her husband.

We saw a few teenage kids who were facing major surgeries or treatments in the coming days. Their parents may have had a more challenging job to support the occasionally moody teens and help them deal with all the pressures of adolescence. I know the Delaware house family advocate got involved and worked to help the families during their hospitalizations and with the transitions back to school. We did speak to some of these parents, and they admitted being overwhelmed by the stress and need to "take a break."

Parents often discussed battles with health insurance companies on paying for treatment, programs available to cover costs when insurance funds ran out, and which doctors, nurses, or social workers were most helpful. Many days they looked like roadkill, with tired eyes, sad frowns, and looks of dishevelment. Other days, when, for instance, a scan came indicating the absence of tumors, they seemed uplifted. The house volunteers were almost all females who got to know the families and provided emotional support.

There were only five full-time staff members and hundreds of volunteers, as I've said. The house's walls were lined with plaques from kids who had recovered from illnesses, and in some cases, rooms were dedicated to kids who had not survived the ordeal. Their families still were grateful to the Ronald McDonald House of Delaware. I secretly hoped and planned to present a plaque one day to the house to reflect our family's gratitude. I also would like to share one with the nurses and therapists at the hospital to celebrate Shannon's successful journey.

Jan volunteered to prepare a turkey dinner for the house one night. She made a list of supplies one morning, and they were there that afternoon. She expertly cooked the turkey, potatoes, and stuffing, which all forty families enjoyed. I invited my mom, dad, and sister Kate for dinner. They loved it, and it was great to have a near-normal visit like this. Kate was overstimulated by the dessert spread and had to take a break. I had spent lots of time while growing up working with Kate on recreational activities and anything to keep her active. My mom said all the time I had spent with Kate was valuable preparation for the challenges I now faced with Shannon.

Jan benefited from the interaction with the other families. I was less willing to discuss our situation with people I barely knew, but I did lean hard on the staff. The multicultural residents of the house made for some diverse cooking in the kitchen. Jan would contribute to their international recipes based on her world travels and culinary expertise. Her presence became a source of comfort for them. We would never have met any of these people if we had commuted from home or stayed at the hospital around the clock. Cooking and enjoying familiar dinners helped many foreign couples feel more at home at the Delaware house. All cultures experience illness and its associated hardships. The Ronald McDonald House of Delaware was welcoming and supportive to all cultures, ethnicities, and religions.

Shannon with her mom outside the Ronald Mcdonald House of Delaware during her first visit there. Reused with RMHC permission.

9

TEAM SHANNON STILL GOING STRONG

Monday-through-Thursday therapy sessions continued with Shannon making each transition with her walker. She nailed many sessions, but agitation took over and nothing was accomplished at times. At other times substitute therapists filled in, and they usually could not get Shannon motivated. Shannon missed Nurses Mary and Heather and would rejoice at their brief reunions. Each night Shannon reinforced her stronger motor skills at the Ronald McDonald House of Delaware. She would insist on banging the piano keys as loud as possible. Her cousins' visits became full of interaction, with shared work on coloring, playing catch, reading books, or even pursuing rabbits outside. We pushed things one night and took Shannon to a nearby mall, and she didn't last long. Back at the Ronald McDonald House, we had such a stockpile of resources to deal with agitation, such as the *Clifford the Big Red Dog* and *The Berenstain Bears* video series, both of which I had just discovered.

The patient we met at Cooper who'd lost his leg in a quad accident was discharged. His dad came to pick him up and told me he and his wife had gotten divorced the day before. I had met some other moms who said their husbands dropped them off at DuPont Hospital with their sick child and were never heard from again. Clearly they could not deal with the stress. I was now running around the hospital grounds and continuing to lift weights in the hospital gym when the security guards did not chase me; I hoped this was a sufficient outlet. Getting back to work was also an outlet. I was committed to Shannon's recovery. The neurological psychologist had told me that the kids with the most parental support did the best.

Our second weekend at home was a little smoother than the first. Shannon insisted on drinking the same red juice and promptly vomited. I was able to cut some grass and paint the garage before rolling into work, where I could pull three shifts over the weekend and have more leave to stay with Shannon during next week's therapy sessions. This also meant Jan and Tara had to deal with Shannon's agitation without my support. Shannon spent time with her friend Brian, who, his mom told me, had been struggling to sleep since the accident. I took Shannon to a schoolyard across the street, and we created an impromptu geese-chasing game. Shannon could do such things better now as the DAFO supports were serving their purpose. I was so glad she no longer had the casts. Shannon and I would approach the geese as she reminded me to keep quiet by saying, "Shhhhh." After spotting a target, Shannon would call out, "Dad." Both of us would take off in hot pursuit, and after ten steps, Shannon would be about to buckle. I would pick her up for another twenty yards of the chase. The geese always flapped away, with Shannon's laughter rivaling their quacks.

Shannon also said "up" and her first two-word combinations of "good morning," "ice cream," and "thank you." Her single-word vocabulary had also expanded with utterances of "down" and "funny." I could not wait to tell the ST of this at the next meeting.

The letters I distributed had really helped as I did not have to brief people on Shannon's progress. It was all in print, and I had an updated version each week. We spoke to Nurse Pat of Cooper, who said the letters had made the Cooper Trauma Center PICU staff's day. Perhaps my plan of accenting the positive and eliminating the negative was starting to work.

Early Monday we drove back to DuPont with Shannon alert and vomiting five times. We had *The Best of Barney* musical score playing, which did little to offset the motion sickness. We had a meeting with Team Shannon, and I proudly announced the two-word phrases Shannon had said over the weekend. The ST seemed to not believe me. Shannon was slightly agitated at the start, so I was tossing her stuffed animal cat named Flip around, and he landed on the top ledge of a light fixture. A few minutes later, as we were listening to the STs comment they were not hearing the two-word phrases, Shannon spotted her cat up high and blurted out, "Mom, Flip up there."

Amazing! She had said a four-word phrase as her two-word-phrase abilities were being challenged. That was just what I needed, as I was running on fumes after working thirty-six hours in the last three days, then driving to DuPont.

One of the new goals Team Shannon set was dealing with ataxia, tremors in the hands and feet from the brain injury due to a lack of coordination of muscle movements. Shannon no longer needed the casts. The DAFOs kept her feet straight. Her hands would shake, which was noticeable when she used a pen, a crayon, or a spoon, fork, or knife. As usual, the therapists said such damage was typically permanent and Shannon would have to learn to deal with it. The OT came up with all sorts of drills like making bead necklaces, grabbing and throwing balls of small dimensions but heavier weight, and doing more-challenging puzzles.

The neurological psychologist got to be one of our favorite people. Some sessions were with Shannon and some with just Jan and me. She answered my questions about the brain. Everything I was reading was negative, with brain injuries being so serious and almost all leaving permanent damage. Dr. Phyllis replied that what I was reading was based on dated treatment models of leaving the patient in bed to rest for months on end. The new approach was to start aggressive therapy programs with patients getting as much stimulation as they could tolerate. She cautioned me about pushing

Shannon too hard, as she was only three years old and was maxed out on therapy. She would describe what regions of the brain controlled cognitive or motor skills, explaining that all the progress Shannon was making was great, but real challenges were ahead with the school system and Shannon dealing with behavior and anxiety issues.

I asked about a patient who seemed perfectly fine walking around the rebab wing. She could not give me details but said she was far from fine, that her injuries impacted her judgment and learning ability. That patient later caused a hospital lockdown when she went missing, having dreamed up an elaborate breakout with an unknowing maintenance man and a drive to Florida. Even Nurse Mary had had to assist. Fortunately, she was located promptly.

Dr. Phyllis also explained possible long-term impacts many faced, such as extreme anxiety or the opposite, no motivation. These sessions gave us some guidance from a subject matter expert and helped us stay focused. Dr. Phyllis repeatedly said that the kids with the most family support did the best.

Shannon's ST since her arrival had left DuPont, and her male replacement was into machines and gadgets that did not help. Her vocabulary was quickly expanding with a new ability to count up to five in OT sessions and some descriptions like "hot," "cold," "cupcake," and "everything."

We were getting frustrated with Shannon's frequent bouts of agitation. The experts said she should move past it at some point. Dr. Phyllis and Nurse Mary and PT Monica kept telling us it was a good sign that she was displaying frustration, which was expected. They would know, as they did this for a living. Team Shannon had done great things already, and we trusted them to continue doing so.

Shannon hard at work in a PT session on a tricycle,
providing a ride for one of her many stuffed animals

10

EMBRACING THE AGITATION

We noticed that Shannon was stronger each weekend and able to do more at home, but her agitation seemed to increase. We took her to the park to continue the pursuit of wildlife. Working to locate the squirrels, rabbits, and ducks helped keep Shannon calm. Feeding them gave her satisfaction. I had to be walking her at least five miles each weekend morning on these trips to the park seeking stimulation prior to going to work in the afternoon. Jan and Tara had to entertain her the rest of the day without the resources of the Ronald McDonald House. We had lots of visitors during this time who were eager to help, but Shannon was rarely interested in engaging. Nurse Mary and the neurological psychologist had told us the agitation was a good sign, as kids who did not go through it had slower recoveries.

I took Shannon to the supermarket, and she immediately mumbled and pointed toward the back of the store where the seafood was. She guided me right to the lobster tank, where the lobsters were swimming around prior to being sold off. Watching the lobsters had been one of her favorite activities prior to the accident. Seeing her remember this was another encouraging sign. She would laugh as they displayed their own forms of agitation with taped claws and scrambling movement throughout the tank. Shannon added "eggs" to her vocabulary when we were in that section. After a half hour, she started crying and pointing toward the exit. I wondered if she felt frustrated at not being able to walk around the store and comment as she used to.

Back home Shannon would play with her friend Brian but would still get agitated after about an hour. Brian had a border collie named Tosh that looked a little like Kirby. He provided some relief but did not have the training Kirby had to encourage kids to play. Shannon could now crawl up the stairs with limited support. She resumed the upstairs-downstairs drill she had started on the first weekend home for hours on end. Fortunately the weather was nice, and we could include the swing set outside in the calming routine.

Back at DuPont on Monday, Shannon made a gigantic leap by saying forty-two words, mainly responding to cards with pictures of common objects. Monica and Cindy of PT and OT, respectively, had her walking around the gym with well-designed treasure hunts so she could rest after about ten steps.

I resumed working on three-point shots on the basement court that was adjacent to the gym. By now the security guards knew me and decided there was no need to chase me off the premises. They preferred I play basketball to working out in the employee gym.

I would occasionally join Jan at the Ronald McDonald House but lacked the discipline to avoid the cookies and danishes and always took my share. On one such visit, we ran into Alex's grandmother, who was celebrating Alex finally getting scheduled for a liver transplant, for which he had waited for ten months. They'd spent the entire time at the house, as they were from Puerto Rico. His color was unhealthy, and his pain was obvious during that time. His grandma had struggled with the extended stay. She gave Jan credit for helping her pray and keeping hope that all would work out.

Marge the family advocate and Karen the director had asked if I could give some speeches on behalf of the house on its role in Shannon's recovery. I replied I would be glad to as their role had been gigantic and increasing awareness of this organization could only help.

After Shannon's first three hours of therapy, she usually took a nap in a nearby lounge. One day it was occupied, so I took Shannon to the hospital chapel, and she promptly fell asleep. Sitting in the chapel with her was awesome, as most of my previous visits had been solo sessions ending in tears. Shannon had made incredible progress, so I thanked God for the results and blessings.

The next transition was to move completely home and make the daily commute to DuPont. Shannon had improved on motion sickness, reducing vomiting to once per trip. I found a route that minimized hills and only added a few miles to the trip. The plan was to commute to DuPont and back Monday through Friday. I would then work a shift from 3:00 to 11:00 p.m. It would leave us exhausted, but we were used to it by now. Shannon had started to enjoy the ride with her Disney tapes playing loudly. She recalled where we had driven past horses and cows on the journey and would look for them.

Upon returning home one Friday, I found eighteen medical bills in the mailbox that represented expenses from Cooper and DuPont. They included ambulance service, x-rays for images and radiological review, medication, IVs, and therapy services. The list went on and on. Insurance would cover them but was not always timely. I dropped off Shannon and Jan and rolled out to work. Neighbors were noticeably starting their weekend with cocktails in the driveway, discussing home-improvement projects or weekend college football games. They also had a fire pit going. It crossed my mind to join them and burn the stack of medical bills. This routine of traveling back and forth to DuPont was not easy, but all I could do was drive on and focus on Shannon's remarkable progress. There were kids who were never going to go home and dads whose kids had conditions that they could not impact. Shannon's brain could recover more quickly with the stimulation and support we provided.

I arrived at work on time and was relieved to see there was a delay in the next flights scheduled to arrive. I took the stack of medical bills and started to review them. Many were for medical treatment that the insurance company would cover. Many bills were also duplicates of what had been previously sent. Surely they would keep sending the same bills until payment was received. I found a nearby shredder and inserted every bill into the feed tray. Listening to the loud sound of the paper being cut into hundreds of small strips felt liberating. Coworkers asked what I was shredding and why it was so enjoyable. I gave them the short reply, "Nothing important." I continued the exercise by removing the bagful of shredded-medical-bill confetti and delivering it to the maintenance man. Perhaps this mission symbolized the thrill of having control in a world where we really had none.

I noticed that during my working hours, I got better ideas about new exercise routines for Shannon or plans for more cognitive activities. I would write them down frantically. Coworkers asked what I was writing and got a standard reply: "Today's therapy progress. Tomorrow's therapy goals."

The following Monday Shannon was eager to get started in an ST session. I had taken pictures of our home and places and people Shannon had liked to encourage her to say more for the ST. She said at the start of her next ST session, "Mom, go away; leave me in speech."

Another trick we suggested for use in sessions was recording Shannon on video and telling her Aunt Tara or her friend Brian was watching. This encouraged her to work harder. She responded by adding some flair by waving while riding a bicycle or speaking to the camera. We hoped this was helping Shannon to use more systems of her brain. We applied the video at home as Shannon would watch the videos of herself and tell others the names of her therapists and activity: "Bike with Monica," "Kitchen with Sandra," or "Nurse Mary back."

Shannon's memory seemed to be intact. She was evaluated and found to have the vocabulary of a two-year-old, which we were content with.

I was still an active member of the US Army Reserves and had missed the last drill weekend. The unit chaplain had visited us at the hospital with cards and well wishes from many coworkers. I returned for the October drill weekend, an officer's staff ride to Valley Forge National Park, where George Washington's forces had spent the winter of 1776. We looked at the terrain and studied Washington's tactics. The chaplain led an impromptu prayer service thanking God for my return to drill weekends and asking for continued blessings on Shannon. It was a beautiful weekend, and I felt almost normal until I called home and Jan described Shannon's high levels of agitation. I wondered how I would make a three-week training course I had scheduled in Kansas in a few months.

DuPont's staff had suggested I talk to the local school system about the early-intervention program for Shannon, as she clearly needed such formal stimulation to continue making progress. The Washington Township School District was highly regarded and one of the reasons we had settled there. I reached out, and within a few weeks, a school district social worker, learning specialist, and neurological psychologist were visiting DuPont and meeting with Team Shannon to coordinate the transition. Next, they scheduled a home visit to determine Shannon's strengths and weaknesses.

My brother Barry visited with some details on the case he was pursuing against the insurance company of the young driver who had run over Shannon. We actually visited the accident scene, and Jan had to describe to Barry the circumstances of Shannon getting crushed by the SUV. She got through it better than expected. I had forced myself not to focus on the accident, as it could not help. Thank God my brother was a seasoned lawyer accustomed to handling such complex proceedings.

I had drafted a letter of complaint against Dr. Cappuccino at Cooper for his rude responses and demeanor in dealing with us and other parents. The hospital director responded with a letter of apology and ten balloons. He promised to follow up and make any necessary changes. We had been in touch with Nurse Pat, and she said my letter promptly brought needed changes. It felt great to help other parents in the PICU, as that is a painful enough nightmare without such irritants.

After that busy weekend, we returned to DuPont, where Shannon nailed ST by saying, "I did it" and "Look at the sky." Monica took Shannon to the hospital pool for the first time, and she had a productive session of water aerobics. She took a tricycle ride back to her room and to Nurse Mary, and overconfidence resulted in a collision, with Shannon falling off the bike. She was wearing her helmet and did not even cry.

The Ronald McDonald House of Delaware had no vacancy and even had to turn away families. It was capped at forty families. Distance traveled and severity of injuries determined who got to stay there and who had to go to local hotels.

One night Shannon was waiting on Kirby and eager to use her expanded vocabulary to give him instructions such as "Find it" and "Let's go." Shannon started to walk Kirby down the hallway and back as he seemed to break into a sweat. What a contrast this was with a few weeks ago, when Kirby was really supporting Shannon on the walk. Shannon also told him to jump lots of times as she held the Hula-Hoop sideways, giving him the target. Kirby seemed to recognize his handiwork, and the two of them were inseparable for a half hour. Kirby had other kids to entertain who were more in need of pet therapy, so we held Shannon back as she watched Kirby go back to basics.

Monica the PT was making the most progress among the members of Team Shannon and told us that it was time to transition Shannon from a walker to a cane. She also developed a falling-down drill in anticipation of Shannon's falls so she would learn to fall on larger muscles and not put her hands down to brace herself. Monica was right to ban us from the sessions and delivered on her promise to provide positive results. Shannon continued to demonstrate new skills after the PT sessions. These included throwing a ball like a pro or showing us objects she had acquired that were strategically placed to make Shannon work to find them. We had some real luck in finding a PT like Monica at DuPont and having my sister Anne as a consultant.

Halloween was fast approaching, and every therapist used it to motivate the kids in their sessions. In ST Shannon was proudly cutting outlined images of pumpkins with scissors while she said "pumpkin" and "orange." In OT Shannon was separating small goblins by color, the first time she had gotten her colors down. In PT Shannon would locate and transport pumpkins of all shapes and sizes. The therapists dressed up in costumes one day and had a parade with the kids around the second floor of the hospital. Jan had a plan to make Shannon a mermaid on Halloween and had started to assemble the outfit.

The Ronald McDonald House of Delaware had an amazing array of Halloween decorations. A volunteer group had donated up to one hundred pumpkins and decorated them with faces, hats, and outfits and created a nation of different pumpkins. The house staff had provided pumpkins for the kids to decorate. This fun activity resulted in fifty more pumpkins joining the display. We wondered if Shannon would enjoy trick-or-treating, as it was a lot of activity and stimulation she might not be ready for.

The next weekend home, I took Shannon to a farmers market with a hayride to the pumpkin patch and an obstacle course of haystacks. She had a great time participating in the hayride and pumpkin selection and climbing around the haystacks. I was hoping to catch some of the Mets versus Yankees Subway World Series but missed most of the games due to my constant working with Shannon. I was also missing the weekly Penn State and Philadelphia Eagles games but was fine with that. Shannon still required activity and entertainment to prevent an increase in agitation.

She took brief breaks to watch her Disney classics, but her attention span was very short.

We attended my nephew's birthday party with Shannon, who blended in with her older cousins and their Barbie doll collections beautifully. All were thrilled to hear her talking more and walking around the house, even if supported by DAFOs. Shannon kept asking my sister, "Where are the pumpkins?" Shannon expected all houses to have a Ronald McDonald House of Delaware level of decorations.

Shannon's mermaid costume was quite impressive, with textures, colors, and a design that made her look like a live mermaid. The tail was at the back of Shannon's feet, which enabled her to walk freely. The neighbors invited Shannon for group trick-or-treating. Shannon could not keep up and fell a few times. I carried her to the houses, then let her walk the last ten steps. Shannon proudly said, "Trick or treat" and "Thank you" before walking back to me to be carried. She lasted the hour we had hoped and wanted to continue. My arms were shot from carrying her, so I grabbed the wagon so we could continue to another block of houses. Upon finishing, Shannon stayed outside and gave out candy to older trick-or-treaters. Her laughter at silly costumes was the perfect climax to a great Halloween.

As promised, we visited the PICU at DuPont with an alert and ambulatory Shannon. The staff quickly recognized her and asked for an update on her progress. The attending and resident physicians were flabbergasted when we described her progress. Dr. Narajavo, the PICU attending physician who had been the first to treat Shannon upon arrival, asked if she was walking. I told Shannon to walk to the nurses' station and back, and she responded with no hesitation whatsoever.

"That is absolutely unbelievable," said Dr. Narajavo, who looked more shocked than he sounded. He went on to say that the test and exam results upon arrival were so grim they did not expect any significant recovery. He also said he was glad all of us had gotten her promptly to rehab, where such miracles can occur. The priority in intensive care is to stabilize the patient so they survive. Rehab shifts the priority to recovery, and that is where kids show real resiliency. The PICU nurses had found time to keep track of Shannon in rehab, so they were not surprised. They just said that we must be sleeping better. I made a note to take Shannon to visit the Cooper PICU as soon as we could.

Shannon's G-tube was scheduled to be removed. She was eating well, and there was no reason to maintain it. The nurse practitioner surprised us with another test that had to be done to see if the tube could be pulled or had to be removed in a more formal setting under anesthesia. Jan was fired up, as we had not been told of this possibility. The test turned out fine, and the tube was removed. We had to hold Shannon still as they yanked it out. We had become accustomed to holding Shannon down, as during her in-patient hospital stay, the staff had drawn blood every couple of weeks after the arterial line was removed and had had trouble finding a vein. It took Jan, Tara, and me to hold her still while she cried. I was glad that was over.

Another army reserve drill weekend arrived; I attended and learned more details about a mandatory three-week course in Kansas in January. The course was required for promotion to major, and if I did not attend, I would be forced out of the service as part of the post–Cold War military drawdown. This would result in no additional income and tighten my recently stretched budget due to medical expenses. I would miss the camaraderie as well. I could not attend, as Shannon still needed daily support and benefited from a maximum amount of stimulation. The new unit commander suggested I ask for an extension.

Jan called me with an agitated Shannon, who would not put on her orthopedic foot braces. She was still very restless when I got home that night; the usual Play-Doh and LEGO diversions were not working. I took her to the Blockbuster video store, and she would not get out of the car.

It was dark and raining, so I could not take her to the park for recreation. She had no interest in movies or arts and crafts activities. I took her to her friend Brian's house, where she played with him and his dog. I had become accustomed to resorting to more than ten options in order to chase the agitation. It did become exhausting, but it was necessary. Military training had taught me to prepare for all contingencies. One night I resorted to shaving cream. I let Shannon decorate the walls and apply it to some stuffed animals and dolls with hilarious results. Thank God Jan was asleep.

The next day at drill, the new colonel assembled the officers and grilled them on lax standards. I had to explain marksmanship standards that had been lacking going back years prior to me joining the unit. I explained they had vastly improved since I had come aboard, but I would take the hit. He replied that was not necessary—as the colonel, he was ultimately responsible. A colleague spoke up and said, "Colonel, I worked with Captain Mulhern a few years ago in Germany; he is pretty good at taking hits." The room erupted in laughter, which was what was needed.

I had always done what I thought was right regardless of political pressure. This approach had gotten me in jams with some high-ranking people who wanted stats padded or drastic implementations to always be successful. While the army was not working out as a primary or backup career, it had prepared me for the demons of dealing with traumatic brain injury. The grind of the Eleventh Armored Cavalry Regiment on active duty was worth it. Shannon did better at home on Sunday, barely noticing my absence.

We were all set to start a Monday-through-Thursday early-intervention program at the school district. Shannon would be picked up by bus at our house and attend three hours of school. The trips to DuPont were scaled back to every Friday. We would stop at Ronald McDonald House of Delaware and pick up some breakfast. Shannon was now in charge of the cookies-for-critters drill. We actually walked from the house to the hospital for the first time. Shannon would drop the snacks at strategic locations, hoping the squirrels responded or possums came up from subterranean tunnels. This gave her the rest she needed every twenty or thirty yards.

Monica started taking Shannon to a sensory room that had more-challenging activities with heavier balls to pick up and throw and challenging swings. Cindy and Sandra, the OTs, had started using water pistols in therapy, and Shannon would ambush me at the end of the session and laugh her head off at her accurate results. I had brought in several books for the ST, who would try to get Shannon to describe the activity page by page. Shannon did better than expected. These were the same books I had read to her when she was in a coma.

On the walk back to the Ronald McDonald House, we found some stray cats. Shannon insisted we get some milk and feed them. This became a weekly activity. I had to remember to grab some small milk cartons from the Ronald McDonald House in the event we ran into the cats. Shannon was worn out by then, so I had to carry her back to the house, but her focus was impressive. She relayed the stray-cat-milk story to all with a level of speech that neared preaccident abilities. While her vocabulary was rapidly expanding, Shannon's voice was breathy and raspy. She had vocal cord paralysis in one cord. This may have occurred when she was intubated on the helicopter ambulance flight or may have been a result of the brain injury. The experts said this was irreversible damage and Shannon would always have such a voice.

On another walk from the Ronald McDonald House to DuPont, Shannon spotted a worker on the roof and said, "Dad, what is that guy doing up there?"

He heard Shannon and replied that he was fixing the alarm. Her voice must have been getting stronger and her peripheral vision better to spot the worker and for him to hear her question.

It crossed my mind that Shannon's raspy voice could be an issue once her peers got to the age of noticing differences and teasing classmates. I put such thoughts in the parking lot. The STs said there were some breath-control strategies Shannon could learn when she was older to help.

I was frequently worn out from the daily grind and would occasionally fall asleep in the chairs outside the rehab gym. Shannon could not resist that opportunity. She would plan an ambush of waking me up with cups of water, which were tossed over my head, or a mountain of stuffed animals. The therapists made her plan a more subtle approach, such as getting a toy spider and stuffing it down my shirt. I would play along like I was shocked and terrified, and Shannon and the staff would laugh their heads off. That was definitely a win-win—I caught a nap, and Shannon planned her attack and got results.

On the car ride back from DuPont, Shannon would take a nap. Finally I could turn off the Barney or Disney music and play some rock and roll. One of my favorite albums was the *Abbey Road* classic from the Beatles. One day "Octopus's Garden" was playing, and Shannon woke up and said they were singing about fish. That was an impressive connection, so her cognitive skills were improving. She also said to put Barney back on. Not bad for a three-year-old's mind.

*Shannon located a squirt water bottle
and started to spray us with no hesitation whatsoever*

11

PRESCHOOL RELIEF

All was set to start Shannon in preschool. We took her for a visit, and the teacher got Shannon involved with circle time and the daily weather forecast. Shannon was assigned a one-on-one aide to help her get around and keep up with the material. She also was assigned a PT for two sessions a week. An ST scheduled one solo session and one group session in class a week.

We left Shannon in class and met with the local version of Team Shannon. They raved about the program DuPont provided and said they were maintaining the system of goal setting and tracking. They had a thick individual education program (IEP) put together in a folder that reflected the goals and covered cognitive areas as well as fine and gross motor skills. We had questions, and they had answers. Clearly the visit they'd made to DuPont was a great start. We felt confident they would maintain an organized and effective program that would meet Shannon's needs. School was local and so much more convenient than DuPont's medical-based format.

Shannon boarded the bus on day two and was eager to get started. The bus was the smaller van type with an aide to watch the kids. Shannon returned home on day two with a small apple pie she had made in school. She also had a daily written update the teachers provided on what the class had worked on so we could reinforce those skills at home. It was always sequencing letters and numbers, basic concepts of time and weather, or other simple facts. There were nine kids in the class with a special education teacher, her assistant, aides for three kids, and usually an ST—a staff of six for nine students. All of the kids had some type of learning disability, but it was not noticeable in most.

Shannon was proud to show us the arts and crafts projects she completed. Her teachers would send home daily updates that reflected that Shannon was all smiles, especially at music time.

Preschool was in session four days a week. On Friday we returned to DuPont Hospital for sessions with the original Team Shannon. Each week was like a reunion, with Shannon happy to return to such familiar territory. She usually slept on the way to DuPont, which helped prevent motion sickness. Shannon brought pictures of her new teachers, aides, and classmates to show the DuPont therapists. This was yet another cognitive activity that made her think. The therapists usually complimented Shannon on her outfits or hairstyles as she proudly showed them slight changes each week. She greeted the therapists with smiles, hugs, and questions on the day's activity. They were overjoyed to hear of the smooth transition to school, as not all had thought she was ready and they had had patients who'd really struggled in the past.

After three grueling hours, we visited the Ronald McDonald House of Delaware. It was nice to be a visitor and not a resident. We saw some of the same families and many new ones with kids facing life-threatening medical situations. It was particularly devastating to see parents who had more than one child afflicted with cancer or another crippling disease. Their strength was very impressive. Many commented on how they used what they learned in their first round against cancer to make the second one easier. All missed Shannon but were glad that she was doing so well.

The reduction of trips to DuPont enabled us to get some much-needed rest. We still worked with Shannon several hours a day. School activities tired Shannon out, so she napped in the afternoon. Things were progressing at a more comfortable pace. Medical bills were flowing in nonstop, but I decided not to worry, as my auto and health insurance policies were not yet depleted. My brother Barry had told us he was not making any progress with the driver's insurance company regarding a negotiated settlement. He said he was looking for a lawyer who specialized in such cases to proceed with the lawsuit against the driver who had run over Shannon. Perhaps his insurance policy would be needed to pay for all of this expensive treatment. More to worry about down the road.

On Fridays at DuPont, while Shannon was in therapy, I regularly went to the Ronald McDonald House of Delaware and gave speeches to corporate-type groups that visited to learn about the house's role and about volunteer programs. Marge reached out to me about speaking at the annual volunteer dinner, which recognized all the volunteers, the true backbone of the house. I could not say no to her and anticipated a crowd of about fifty people. There must have been two hundred people there, with no drinks available to warm me up.

I felt nervous with such a large crowd and expected the butterflies in my stomach. I had started slamming cheese crackers when the board president called us up to the front. I started giving details of Shannon's injuries and the house's role in her recovery. I was speaking off the top of my head and appeared to be doing well without rehearsal. Shannon seemed to like the attention as she and Jan were in the front but off to the side. I could see most people looking at her. I gave credit to the staff members, cooks, decorators, flower ladies, pet therapy handlers, bikers in attendance who ran toy drives for the kids, landscapers, and maintenance men. I was on a roll. I found myself looking at Marge; Karen, the house director; and a few other full-time house employees whom I knew. Familiar faces can relax you when you're speaking to a large crowd. I described how the house's resources and volunteers had helped Shannon make major progress in a short period of time. Jan finished up by addressing the family atmosphere of the house. There were few dry eyes left. I wrapped it up to a loud round of applause. The president of the Delaware house board of directors thanked us by saying, "That was such a powerful story." He continued the program by recognizing many long-serving volunteers.

Afterward I was surprised by the compliments that came our way. Kirby's handler's husband, who took pictures of Kirby with the kids, said he had attended many such events and found my speech to be the best. Female members of the board said I perfectly captured what the house was all about and moved them to tears. Another board member told me of her son who did not survive a cancer battle but fought so bravely they donated the statue of him outside in honor of all kids in similar battles. Others approached me and said they, too, had been medical miracles not expected to survive rooftop falls or severe illnesses but who somehow overcame the scientific facts. That speech became a reference point in my mind to replace the dark days and long nights of intensive care.

It felt good to give something back to the Ronald McDonald House. They provided real results and kept us together so we did not become one of the statistics I read about on divorce, bankruptcy, and so on. People have said I have a unique and effective speaking style. All of those safety briefings, operations orders, and road-march briefings I gave in the army have paid off. Keeping soldiers motivated when they were cold, wet, tired, and hungry was never easy, but it prepared me for that night. Some of the other training I received while on active duty had given me confidence that I could work long hours in stressful conditions and stay focused on a positive outcome. Shannon's recovery to date had required all the managerial and motivational tools I had ever learned. Perhaps I had a future career in motivational speaking.

I kept thinking about how families could deal with all the challenges of traumatic brain injury without the support of the Ronald McDonald

House. We had a case of PediaSure, which provided extra nutrition to young kids and was commonly used by youngsters with G-tubes for direct nourishment. Shannon was well past this stage, so I decided to give it to the young boy who nearly drowned. I delivered it to his mom at her residence in Pennsauken, New Jersey, which is about thirty-five miles from DuPont Hospital. The town had a few riverfront piers I was familiar with from arriving cargo vessels. She showed me where her son had gone into the pool after the dog, then gotten stuck and nearly drowned. Responding medics treated him and took him to the hospital promptly. His mom was commuting back and forth to DuPont with her son as an inpatient. She continued this commute after he was discharged to daily therapy. I described all the Ronald McDonald House of Delaware had to offer, and she was not interested. His dad relocated somewhere in California after this family tragedy. His son and wife deserved better.

We stayed at the house the night after the volunteer-recognition event as Shannon's weekly scheduled sessions at DuPont were the next day, Friday. Shannon was sharper mentally that morning and able to comment on whatever we ran into. She spotted a window washer in the hallway and said, "Look at that guy." She spotted her tricycle in the hallway and said, "Why is my bike here?"

Shannon carried the energy from the night before to her therapy sessions. In ST she was able to verbally identify all body parts and 80 percent of colors. In OT she told Sandra of the party last night with several four-word phrases, then cut images along very fine lines. In PT Shannon hit the pool with an unprecedented wave of enthusiasm. She actually jumped from the side of the pool to Monica's outstretched arms and was proud of her splash landing. She continued the banner day by holding her breath and going under the water for two seconds. What a therapist Monica was! Monica gave the credit back to Shannon and her courageous attitude in sessions. Another PT saw us and commented on the improvement in Shannon's gait, with reduced inward turning of her feet, or forefoot abduction, as they called it.

The pool workouts helped Shannon's overall balance and core strength. Monica managed to get Shannon comfortable on the stairs, which had been a real challenge. DuPont had a small set of stairs in the rehab gym, which Shannon had mastered months prior. Actual stairs were still difficult. At home Shannon usually sat down and squirmed herself down the stairs, as that technique was much more effective. The pool sessions gave her additional confidence to tackle the stairs and overcome them.

Shannon was able to recall other patients and perk up upon seeing them. It was difficult to see the same kids facing the same medical hardship as the last time we had seen them. Jan had gotten to know their parents and learned the details: some kids had had strokes; for others, anesthesia errors during routine surgeries had led to severe impairment; and other kids had had neurological disorders since birth. Few families were enjoying the great medical strides we were, and our hearts went out to those at a different stage of recovery.

Shannon and Jan at a "parents visit the class" day

12

HOLIDAY RESOURCES

The upcoming Thanksgiving holiday provided more material for the therapists, and Shannon was proudly coloring and cutting turkeys of all shapes and sizes. She had the presence of mind to save them for her schoolteachers and aunts as Thanksgiving gifts. We celebrated Thanksgiving at my sister Betty's house with Shannon impressing all by walking around in pursuit of the cat. She also would stick her tongue out at people and point to her ears, nose, and eyes without being asked. How could she remember that doctors had asked her to do these things several times a day? Anne was impressed with Shannon's mobility and her understanding of basketball and kickball. She asked Shannon where she had learned these games, and Shannon replied, "Evelyn taught me." Evelyn was the school's PT. It was a great Thanksgiving, with everyone excited that Shannon was recovering so quickly after receiving grim diagnoses from the experts at two hospitals.

The colder weather was limiting my outdoor sessions with Shannon. It had dipped to below-freezing temperatures. The ducks and squirrels were nowhere to be found. I did find some bigger rocks and had Shannon toss them onto a slightly frozen pond, with the resulting breakage of ice sending her roaring in laughter. The noise would bring out some ducks from hiding, and Shannon would state, "There they are." Fortunately the stores made up for the inclement weather with Christmas displays, which we visited and admired. Technology had improved the displays with lots of life-size figures of Santa, elves, and reindeer. Holiday music was playing at all malls and stores.

Another frequent destination in the cold weather became the pet store full of dogs, cats, birds, fish, and small creatures. Shannon had to be stopped from walking into the cat enclosure area. The helpful attendants would bring several cats out for Shannon to pet and talk to. They required a sign-in sheet to limit visitors to one visit a month. I used several different names on the sheet to create more opportunities. I had become so familiar with the store that I located a lizard that had escaped the tank and for which the employees had been frantically searching. Shannon found this hilarious.

The mall provided a replacement for the park, as Shannon would walk from heavily decorated stores to the toy store to the bookstore. Such activity increased Shannon's appetite, and she had her choice of snacks at the food court. At times Shannon's agitation returned, and she insisted on being pushed in the stroller. She usually took long naps after her extended walks through the mall.

The preschool seemed to be overdoing it on seasonal arts and crafts. Shannon was happy to bring home paper creations of Santa, elves, and reindeer. She also practiced seasonal songs at home and planned special gifts for classmates. We wanted to show our gratitude to all who had helped us the past six months. We decided to make plaques to give to family members and the rest of Team Shannon. There was a picture of Shannon in her glory after climbing a few stairs at the gym in DuPont with a beaming smile. We chose this photo to put on the plaque with the statement, "'Where there is faith, there are miracles.' Thanks for your efforts, which brought Shannon from the brink of death to a miraculous recovery in the fall of 2000."

I located a friendly vendor in north Philadelphia and got fifty plaques made for a reasonable price. Shannon presented some of the plaques herself to the staff of professionals. We gave one to Nurse Mary and the rest of the nursing staff. We gave another to the PT staff. We gave another to the Ronald McDonald House of Delaware, and they promptly posted it on the wall by the main entrance. The rest went to family, neighbors, and friends who had supported us with prayers, visits, meals, rides, and so forth. We wrapped about half of them for opening on Christmas, which made an unforgettable gift. Giving out the plaques was an exhilarating experience. Some recipients broke down in tears of happiness. It was a form of creating a positive memory after a series of jolting negatives.

We planned the trip back to Cooper Trauma Center with a plaque at a time when Nurse Pat and Dr. Murza were working. Shannon walked in and continued walking to the wide-open arms of Nurse Pat. She hugged Shannon and thanked her for making her dream of Shannon returning healthy come true. Dr. Murza was just as happy to see Shannon, even though she was reluctant to go to him. The nurses made a fuss over Shannon as they arrived quickly from different departments. Dr. O'Conner, the trauma surgeon, got word and came to see the good news. He looked more shocked than anyone. He was the first physician to treat her and the one who'd given us the devastating briefing that included the hypothesis that it may take months for Shannon to wake up. He commended us for doing so much to help her recover. *How does he know all that we did? We have had no contact with him. Perhaps Nurse Pat has kept him informed.*

Dr. Murza asked me what my feelings were upon returning to Cooper. I said they were feelings of gratitude and achievement. He said he understood my frustration with some of the issues we'd had. He said he recalled seeing the bruising on Shannon's brain on the MRI and knew of the slim odds of recovery, but his gut feeling told him that Shannon was a girl who could recover. He said he rarely shared a gut feeling with parents but had done so in our case. He spoke of the many patients he had sent to DuPont, with most of them having done well. He pointed out an eight-year-old boy in the PICU with a similar injury to Shannon's whose father was severely injured in a car accident and could not provide the support I had given Shannon. Both Dr. Murza and Dr. O'Conner thanked us for visiting with Shannon, as they rarely got to see patients out of intensive care. Jan hugged both physicians and promised to keep them informed of Shannon's progress. Dr. Murza told us he would be leaving Cooper for a position at a hospital in California soon and would hold Shannon as a great inspiration in being a PICU physician.

What do you say to people who saved your daughter's life? They are dedicated professionals who did their job, and I resolved to treat whomever I encountered in my profession well and to help families in similar circumstances if I could.

Shannon was busy walking around the PICU modeling her long hair. She saw a baby in a bed connected to lots of tubes and seemed worried. She asked, "Will the baby be OK?"

A female doctor whom I did not remember from Shannon's stay said, "This makes it all worthwhile."

Shannon presented one of her plaques and pointed to a spot high on the wall next to the Christmas tree, suggesting it be hung up there. Nurse Pat was happy to oblige. Shannon also gifted cookies she had helped make to the nursing staff. She gave out more hugs to the tearful staff, and we were on our way. I wondered about the other patients and their challenging paths ahead. Would they get to DuPont or another facility with the same level of care and successful treatment we had experienced?

The parents had their own injuries to overcome, which made a smooth transition impossible. Social workers would help. On our next trip to DuPont, I saw the social worker who had facilitated Shannon's transfer and managed her case at DuPont. She was starting the same with several patients at Cooper. She was at Cooper after our visit and said the staff was glowing about Shannon's visit.

We made holiday greeting cards with a picture of Shannon outside the Ronald McDonald room at DuPont Hospital, with a magnificent grin, holding her white stuffed dog. Uplifting trees and sky images were painted on the background wall, and Shannon was standing proudly. The caption read, "Miracle Girl 2000." I got one hundred copies made and included a newsletter with Shannon's latest accomplishments, including her successful transition to school. Shannon single-handedly delivered them to neighbors' mailboxes and was in her glory delivering to all of Team Shannon. Such activities were helpful to all as we were creating memories beyond the intensive care nightmares and long struggle with agitation.

Many kids did not have such good news to share, as they were still struggling with the brain injury demons. Aside from the medical issues, families faced financial hardship, career interruption, marital stress, and daily exhaustion. I felt as though we were climbing out of the getting back to home/school/work struggle after surviving the trauma/hospitalization/prognosis phase. I wondered at times, *Is a full recovery from a severe traumatic brain injury possible?* No need to think long range. I tried to focus on the present and what I could do to help Shannon recover.

Shannon received countless gifts that holiday season. Some allowed her to expand her vast Barbie collection; others, like decorative beads to string and challenging pictures to color, enabled her to continue work on OT activities. She enjoyed computer discs of her favorite Disney characters at work or play, and a new collection of Play-Doh was a great invention to work hands and calm agitation. The *Pocahontas* computer game was her favorite, as she had to find the critters on screen. Once located, they jumped up and ran to join the princess. These activities worked on vision, hand-eye coordination, and decision making, so they were exercising several systems of the brain. *Clifford the Big Red Dog* was another favorite computer game. Shannon helped Clifford pull items from his house and choose proper items from a store. The program would give hints when Shannon made mistakes and direct her to better choices. Once successful, she was rewarded with a fresh image of Clifford to paint or color with a vast array of colors. She knew how to print out the prize and show everyone. What technology!

The Ronald McDonald Houses of the Philadelphia Region added to the holiday celebration as spectacularly as it had supported us the past six months. They planned a trip to the Philadelphia airport for a simulated plane ride to the North Pole and a party with special guests. They reached out to British Airways for the airplane and needed a US Customs representative to facilitate airport access and coordinate resources. Guess who was a willing US Customs representative? I was available and eager to work with the airline, airport, and house to set up a winter wonderland for one hundred sick kids.

Kids from each of the three area Ronald McDonald Houses were taken by bus to the airport. They checked in to a British Airways flight and taxied around the runway with departure and arrival to the North Pole announcements. A full flight crew served the kids refreshments. Upon returning to the gate, they entered into an area decorated as the North Pole with snow, Christmas trees, large wrapped presents, gigantic candy canes, and an impressive light display. Live immigration officers processed the kids as arriving passengers and stamped the passports that had been specially created for the occasion. Volunteers were dressed as elves, and they prepped all the kids for the arrival of Santa Claus, who distributed age-appropriate gifts.

A US Customs canine team gave a demonstration, with yours truly describing the process of how dogs screened people at airports for narcotics. The pinnacle of the event was children's entertainer David Jacks performing a musical show in which he made the parents participate, closing with his classic tune "Snow in the Summertime." All the kids, including some in wheelchairs and some with no hair from chemotherapy, had a great time. I knew of a few additional kids from DuPont who could not attend due to advanced illnesses. The adult volunteers seemed to have as much fun as the kids.

The event wrapped up around 5:00 p.m. as the kids reboarded the buses to return to the Ronald McDonald Houses. I got to talk to the airport and British Airways organizers, who were in their glory. They raved about what a rewarding experience it was to bring a few hours of happiness to children facing medical nightmares. They thanked me for the Customs coordination and said they hoped to make this an annual event. Nine months later the 9/11 attacks occurred, and airport security changed forever.

New Year's Day brought eight inches of snow and a real workout for Shannon as she helped me shovel. She lasted ten minutes, then suggested we make a snowman. I was surprised at her ability to maintain balance while walking in the snow. She also spotted a neighborhood cat missing his tail and said, "What happened to the cat's tail?" So her vision was fine. She was exhausted after two hours of snow play and took a long nap. The nap enabled her to stay up to ring in the New Year by watching fireworks on TV. We had missed the Fourth of July fireworks, so seeing them together on New Year's felt great.

I still had leave remaining so was able to take time off during Shannon's break from school and run stimulating cognitive activities all day. Shannon would participate with great enthusiasm. After a few hours, she would tire and request a Disney movie. Disney's deep arsenal of movies didn't disappoint, and *The Lion King* and *The Aristocats* were her latest favorites. I did not want her to get much of a respite, as we had to keep working to connect the neurons in her brain that had been separated or twisted from her injury. I had read several books on brain injury by now that advocated frequent stimulation. They also were full of bad news and grim prognoses for anyone who had suffered a diffuse axon injury. Shannon's recovery was a classic case of neuroplasticity, or the brain's ability to reorganize itself by forming new neural connections. The capacity of the brain to recover from injury was starting to get some national press, especially in the context of older people who had had strokes and were encouraged to take dance lessons to enhance their recovery.

My army reserve unit had its annual holiday party, with most soldiers bringing their wives and kids, as the emphasis was on Santa's arrival and gifts. Shannon blended right in, and my colleagues were happy for us. At the start of the day, the unit clerk gave me a formal letter stating that since I did not attend the three-week course in Kansas, which would have qualified me for promotion to major, I was to be separated from the army. The service was still drawing down, and officers were the first to get forced out. There was no way I could have left my daughter while she was in a period of recovery. I had requested an extension, which had been denied. The unit executive leadership was aware and suggested I transition to an enlisted man status, then apply to be a warrant officer. They said they already had letters of recommendation should I choose to appeal, but odds of approval were slim as the only criterion was attending that course. It was a surreal day in light of this grim news. Sergeants not aware of it were reaching out for me to train military police soldiers at the next two drills. Shannon enjoyed the festivities like a normal, healthy person. Her progress was most important, so I enjoyed the moment and buried the rest.

The army's lack of flexibility got me fired up. I considered myself an asset to the unit and someone who always took care of my men while accomplishing the mission. Separation meant the loss of that income from monthly drills and summer training. I had taken skills from the army and applied them to US Customs, to myself, and to other officers. However, the harder I thought about it, the more I accepted it, as the unit was due for an activation overseas that would last up to nine months. The unit was activated several times for a total time of deployment of three and a half years in a five-year period. The events of 9/11 required reserve units to carry a big load in the battle against terrorism. How would Shannon and Jan have fared without me for that long? Could this have been a blessing in disguise?

A few days later, everyone woke up to another surprising eight inches of snow. All the neighborhood kids went sledding on a hill a few blocks away. We joined them with no hesitation whatsoever. I had purchased a larger sled made of a powerful plastic that one of the other parents had recommended as safe but not very fast for the expense. There was plenty of room for me and Shannon as she sat in the front and enjoyed the fast pace down the hill and the continuation of fifty yards onto adjacent fields. She saw small kids sledding themselves and proudly said, "Dad, I want to do it myself."

I supported her plans, glad I had bought the safer sled and she had her bicycle helmet on, and took her to the top of the hill, where I got her in position for a solo run. I positioned myself halfway down to slow her rate of descent. She waved me down to the bottom, stating I was blocking her path. I went to the bottom of the hill, and as I turned around to tell her to push off, Shannon was heading straight for me at a high rate of speed. She was proudly sitting up, her head held high and hands firmly holding on to the sled rope. I jumped sideways as she continued for another twenty yards. She lost control and fell off the sled, splashing snow everywhere. She laughed her head off and yelled, "Dad, I did it myself!"

I ran to her and brushed off the snow. Shannon needed help climbing to the top of the hill but made five additional runs. She wiped out at the end of each one but loved the rush. I was celebrating like a wild man, congratulating her and jumping around. The remaining neighbors, many of whom had called it a day, must have thought I was crazy. Memories like this were replacing the painful memories of the days in the PICU. Experiences like this gave her material to take to school, where she could describe her adventures.

*Shannon showing exuberance prior to
a series of grueling therapy sessions*

13

KNOCKED BACK TO EARTH

Shannon started the new year glad to get back to school and her normal routine. She was eager to take some of her new toys for show-and-tell time. We were happy with her remarkable progress, both physically and cognitively. Her agitated periods occurred less frequently. We were glad for a new year, as the last six months had been so stressful with the accident, hospitalization, devastating diagnosis, months of therapy, daily exhaustion, and the resulting impact on our marriage, jobs, and preaccident life. The worst was behind us as Shannon had recovered and all had rallied around us to help us with the challenges. I was still working with Shannon up to six hours a day on play activities to make her stronger and learning-enhancement drills to help her catch up with her peers. All seemed to be going well. The preschool child study team called us in for a meeting, which had to be an update on how well Shannon was doing.

Shannon's teacher, aide, PT, learning specialist, ST, case manager, and neurological psychologist all sat around the table. Her teacher was the first to speak up.

"Shannon is simply adorable and is all smiles, especially at circle time and music time. She struggles to pay attention during class and seems to drift off into another world. We can reengage her, but this does happen frequently. She is content to sit and watch and watch. We need her to initiate at times."

The ST continued the surprisingly negative progress report.

"We had a story activity in which the kids had to organize pictures of a snowman melting and create a story." The therapist appeared frustrated that her efforts had not been rewarded with results. She continued, "Shannon needed cues to put the pictures in the right sequence. After fifteen minutes of my prodding, her story was 'One, two, three, melt.' She has demonstrated delayed processing and delayed articulation on a daily basis."

The learning specialist was next, with more technical classifications of Shannon's struggles and with plans to introduce goals to keep her focused and find words more easily. The ST resumed speaking. "Shannon interrupts class several times a day with comments on whatever comes to mind. At times her comments are completely off-topic. We were so happy when she said anything at all when she started, but now she has to learn when to speak appropriately."

Talk about being knocked off the mountain back to the valley. Shannon had come so far so fast, but now her preschool team was describing multiple learning disabilities with no easy path to overcoming them. The neurological psychologist at DuPont had warned us not to get too excited with Shannon's progress, as challenges would be with us for years to come. Time to go back to the drawing board and come up with a new game plan.

We did not agree with the negative assessment. Shannon was capable of describing events in order and at times called me with an enthusiastic summation of events at home, such as this memorable description: "Dad, we were in the playroom cutting and coloring, and the doorbell rang. It was some kids, and they asked Mom if she saw my piglet. Mom said, 'Yes, it is roasting out back.' They said, 'Have you seen my guinea pig?' and they ran away. It was so funny. It's called ding-dong ditch it."

Such detailed reporting on events was impressive. We had to get her to articulate similarly in the classroom. As had been the case at DuPont during therapy sessions, she still communicated better at home than in formal settings.

We immediately went to Toys "R" Us and loaded up on learning toys that responded with bells and whistles when the correct choice was made. Technology had come so far with toys that asked questions, then rewarded the right response. Other toys had a recorded voice saying, "Try again" in response to wrong answers. We also got more computer games that had Shannon picking outfits with Disney princesses or counting honey pots with Winnie-the-Pooh. The teachers at DuPont had used such programs. Our focus to this point had been gross motor skills. We had to shift to cognitive skills.

I did some more internet research and found the condition of commenting off-topic was a by-product of the left and right hemispheres of the brain not working together. Activities involving moving both arms and legs simultaneously should help, and this was what the therapists at DuPont had often done. Swimming helped in the summer. I made a note to inquire about whether noncontact karate programs were available for four-year-olds.

I was glad that Shannon had access to professionals who could identify problems and address them. These issues seemed like they were manageable and could be addressed with some direct attention. From the helicopter medics to the trauma center physicians and nurses to the DuPont therapists to the teachers and therapists of the school system, Shannon had been cared for by more than one hundred professionals, all of whom were determined to help her get better. If we kept driving on, we would see continued improvement.

Shannon showed improvements every day in her daily routine. She could get dressed by herself, walk to the school bus in front of the house by herself, brief us on the school activities upon return, get her own snacks in the kitchen, select toys from her vast collection, tell us what videos to play on TV, engage with playmates, and suggest plans for her favorite activities. I told myself to focus on what she was doing, not what she was *not* doing. This philosophy had helped me endure since day one.

As usual I turned to my family and their subject matter expertise. My sister Betty was a grade-school teacher with a master's degree in special education. I explained the recent report of problems with word-finding skills, writing certain letters and numbers, and daydreaming. Betty started working with Shannon on a weekly basis on these specific issues. I insisted she charge us and submitted the invoices to the insurance company, hoping the service was covered.

We looked for books that had mainly pictures and encouraged Shannon to create her own story based on the images. We sought Shannon's opinion on a shopping list and tried to get her to take charge in the food store. We started asking Shannon challenging questions like, "How many animals can you name in one minute?" and "How many colors can you name in ten seconds?" We had Shannon pick out Valentine's cards and plan out whom she would give them to. She mentioned a few classmates and teachers, her best friend, next-door neighbor Brian, and of course Nurse Mary, PT Monica, OT Cindy, and Dr. Ray. Shannon identified which cards would go to which person. She struggled with writing names. She told us she would lick the envelopes closed and give them out. These activities seemed to help, but we needed a Ronald McDonald House event to remind us of how far we had come.

We had agreed to participate in a video about the work the Ronald McDonald House of Delaware did. Several families were featured, with details of their child's injury or illness and the house's role in the recovery. Jan, Shannon, and I were interviewed under professional lights with real makeup applied to reduce the glare. The film crew insisted on interviewing Jan and me separately. Another cameraman followed Shannon and me as she played on the outdoor playground or walked Kirby up and down the halls. My interview included simple questions such as, "Describe your stay at the house" or "What role did the house play in your daughter's recovery?" The end product was quite impressive, with me describing the previously unknown to many resources of the Delaware House amid the recovery process, Jan describing the family atmosphere that gave support, and Shannon looking like a healthy, content child.

The video included the first photos we'd taken of Shannon with an NG tube down her nose, several casts on her limbs, and a very dizzy expression. It also showed Shannon reacting to Kirby from her wheelchair with a gigantic smile on her face while wearing three casts. Then there were shots of Shannon crawling after Kirby without casts and petting him, then of Shannon speaking to Kirby, then of Shannon walking with Kirby. After showing a few more segments on the Delaware House, they went back to shots of Shannon enjoying the swing set with minimal assistance. The video cut to my comments on Shannon's recovery despite the pessimistic prognosis. The ending had a real climax of Shannon holding my hand while walking out of the house and waving back. What a tearjerker! I used the video as encouragement, as we had come so far. Additional academic setbacks were nothing we could not overcome.

The video was shown at the Ronald McDonald House of Delaware tenth-anniversary dinner, which we did not attend. It ran until late at night, and Shannon had a busy-enough schedule. Dr. Ray later told me he saw the video at the dinner, and there was not a dry eye in the place.

Shannon displaying her improving motor skills
by handling a hose like a pro

14

SEEKING RELIEF IN MIAMI

I had to attend a training course in Miami, Florida, and was happy to bring my family to enjoy the warm weather, which had to help Shannon regain focus. We drove there despite some concerns about Shannon's motion sickness. It had improved, especially later in the day, so I did lots of driving in darkness while Shannon slept.

We stayed in a bayfront hotel in a spacious room. Shannon wasted no time in enjoying the warm and sunny weather by hanging out in the lobby in the morning. She loved to talk to dogs that residents were walking to and from an adjacent park. Shannon, Jan, and her teenage niece who joined us blended right in with the fashion models staying at the hotel and the female Hispanic college students at the art school next door. Shannon would dedicate the morning to working on papers from school teaching letters, numbers, colors, shapes, and sizes.

In the afternoon she would go to the pool with her arm floats and get a real workout. Upon my return from training the first day, I found Shannon in the pool proudly boasting, "Dad, I am swimming like a fish in the pool." I was thrilled to join her in the refreshing water and implement some exercises with the water serving as the resistance. Shannon even learned how to carry us in the water aided by the buoyancy and our floating efforts. She would sound off, "I can carry everyone."

Evening crowds arrived, so we moved on. Shannon was ready to roll by the time I got home. I felt worn down, having driven from New Jersey to Florida and attended the challenging training, but was eager to seize the opportunity of Shannon's new stimulating environment. Each night we went to Bayside Marina and enjoyed the live bands as well as the dozens of restaurants, street performers, and unique kiosks. Shannon was in her glory pulling us both down to dance to the salsa-style music and receiving lots of compliments from strangers on her enthusiasm. Her DAFOs were doing their job, enabling her to walk everywhere with straight feet.

There was a merry-go-round and some other entertaining rides for kids. Sidewalk vendors made balloons and displayed their tropical birds. One had a monkey accepting quarters, and others hawked various toys. Shannon got lots of attention from the salesmen as she tried all their gadgets with great enthusiasm. Many people in the crowd seemed to stare at Shannon and smiled as she moved about and commented on all the new items at each station. I wondered if they were speculating about what her medical issue was as they noticed the white braces that ran up her calves.

Jan and I were close behind and relieved she was doing well in a setting where we had expected a meltdown due to overstimulation. We felt as though we were escorting an angel. Older people admired Shannon's persistence and seemed to comment to each other. We could not hear them, but they may have been saying, "If that little girl is working through her injury, we can work through ours too." They started moving more quickly with their canes and walkers. Back at the hotel, Shannon was exhausted from all the walking and fell right asleep.

The next day Shannon was still tired and fell frequently. She also kept asking about "monsters" and pretending she was scared. She must have learned that at preschool. We went to the hotel pool late in the afternoon and decided to stay in and rest after that. There were reports of a gigantic snowstorm with lots of car accidents back in the Northeast. It was great to be here enjoying the warm weather.

The next day Jan took Shannon to SeaWorld while I was at training. We went back to the pool that night, and Shannon was demonstrating all sorts of animal tricks she had seen at SeaWorld.

On the second week, my work schedule shifted to a p.m. shift. This gave me the opportunity to spend mornings with Shannon. She showed me her Miami routine with great passion. First, we went to Burger King for breakfast, then to the park next door, where Shannon would reach out to the same people walking their dogs. Shannon knew it was trick time and started to walk backward for me and the pets. I was impressed with her balance despite the slow pace. This was great material to report to her therapists, as walking backward had been a struggle. Next, she showed me the rock selection bayside and how far she could throw the rocks into the bay. She spotted what appeared to be a gigantic duck in the water and yelled, "Quack, quack."

Next, we went back to the hotel pool, where Shannon introduced me to the lifeguard and some kids she had gotten to know. She got a great workout in thirty minutes. I hated to leave her at noon but had to keep up with the course requirements. Anything I learned in Miami could be applied in the Port of Philadelphia.

The girls continued to visit Bayside Marina at night, and Shannon knew where to go to get her face painted and what vendors would give out balloons. This trip was clearly showing Shannon had a strong memory, and her energy level enabled her to find real enjoyment. Shannon took naps while I was working the p.m. shift. She also worked on her school material in the afternoon. Shannon was getting tired toward the end of the second week. On an evening outing to South Beach, she insisted on being carried. She also started to say, "It's time to go home."

She was absolutely right, as we were worn out. Driving back was even more of a grind, as Shannon got bored. She lacked the energy for our usual antics at truck stops. We still stopped every hundred miles or so and bought a small gadget to keep Shannon entertained. Her favorite was a small stuffed bear that sang Valentine's Day tunes.

It was a great trip—we were able to enjoy Florida weather in the winter and practice new forms of recreation. Such activity was great for our family, as we were creating memories that could offset the recent powerfully painful memories of Shannon struggling in a coma in intensive care. I was fried from the road trip and long days but glad I had found a jump start to help Shannon. What I was doing now meant greater cognitive capacity and easier times in the future.

Shannon marched around the house when we got back, looking for her cat, whom I had taken to one of my sisters. They were reunited the next day, with Shannon briefing her cat on her adventures in Florida and promising not to leave him behind again. She summarized the trip in short comments such as "No cats in Miami, just dogs," "We found the birds and balloons and music at night," "They had a big pool," and "Miami so warm; too cold here."

She was eager to get back to school with her gifts for her classmates of small shark figures from SeaWorld. She was also anxious to get back to DuPont on Friday and explain her work in the park and pool in Florida. She did a full somersault for the first time and was proud of that accomplishment.

On a trip to the pet store, she appeared to be walking faster and told the birds there of all the colorful birds in sunny Florida. Shannon's activities in Florida gave her more things to think and talk about and reduced her agitation at home. We had all the activities she completed in Miami to use when necessary to remind her of what she was able to accomplish. Several weeks later Shannon's teacher commented that Shannon had improved physically and socially since the trip to Florida. *Yes!*

I saw this real progress firsthand when I visited the school on Saint Patrick's Day and saw the kids do a hilarious leprechaun dance. I also read three books to the class, and Shannon had all the answers, as she was familiar with the stories. Her aide commented on how loud the normally quiet Shannon was that day. I was impressed by how the teachers used positive reinforcement to refocus some kids who could not sit still. Some would stand up and walk away before the teacher encouraged them to return and lead the next activity.

Shannon showing her dad how to balance tropical birds in Miami

Shannon enjoying the rides and warm weather in Miami

15

MOTHER NATURE HELPS

Back in New Jersey, spring returned and brought with it the opportunity to resume outdoor exercise. Shannon rode her bicycle with training wheels around the block at a slow but steady pace. I took her to the park so she could ride her bike on some smaller hills that required real effort to ascend. I would walk next to her and pretend to struggle to climb the elevation, which made her laugh and push on. Coming down the hill was more fun. She would stop whenever she saw dogs and reach out. After we moved on, Shannon would ask when we could go back and see Kirby. I made a point to try to schedule some appointments on Monday afternoons, since Kirby was at the Ronald McDonald House of Delaware on Monday evenings.

Shannon also enjoyed hitting Wiffle balls off a tee. She started after the holidays in the house and now needed the backyard, as she could smack line drives up to twenty yards. I even started throwing easy pitches to her. She could make contact at least half of the time. She also was enjoying a small air hockey game that she had struggled with at the beginning. She could now track the puck and whack it. The DuPont therapists also worked with her on a large air hockey game, as it built her stamina through standing and vision and coordination required by following and hitting the puck.

Shannon continued to make steady progress in preschool. Our goal was to have her "mainstreamed" by the time she got to kindergarten. That meant she would be part of the regular curriculum without aides or self-contained classes. The child study team told us this was an unrealistic goal, but what else was new.

We returned to the playgrounds at local parks, where Shannon was happy to display her improved balance. For the first time, I could take a seat while she walked from sliding board to swing and ran throughout the entire area. She could also run in a more coordinated fashion while still favoring her right side, and this looked like a sideways hop. She could even change direction, which she had not been able to do in the fall. The ground was soft mulch, which prevented bruises from Shannon's frequent falls. Shannon must have been practicing games like hide-and-seek at school because she would suggest them in different settings in the park. She could accurately count to twenty and give short descriptions of the games. Shannon was ready for more-challenging entertainment. She had more core strength, which enabled her to go higher on the swings.

One day she was proud of reaching new heights but did not react to other little kids approaching the downward path of the swing. I intervened just in time to prevent the collision. She clearly had limited peripheral vision on her left side. I recalled the neurological ophthalmologist at Du-Pont, saying this could be an issue. Now that Shannon was more mobile and doing more-challenging activities, it was more noticeable. I made a point to schedule her for a checkup. I also planned activities to get her to use her peripheral vision, such as catching balls tossed from various angles, having her track birds way up in the sky, or scanning for objects that were off to the sides.

The roller coaster recovery continued as we would rejoice at the play-ground over her increased activity, yet this led to recognition of yet another medical concern that required attention. We got an appointment within a week with the neurological ophthalmologist. Shannon sensed it was not one of her normal therapy sessions and was very nervous. All normal approaches could not keep Shannon calm. I took her most lifelike doll figures and said they had to get their eyes checked. I told Shannon we were going to visit the nurses after the eye doctor, and she finally settled down. She got a fine report from the doctor, who acknowledged there were limits in her peripheral vision and reaction time, but they had greatly improved since her last exam. She could not tell us if this would be a problem down the road. Shannon got eye drops and had to wait for them to dilate her eyes before continuing.

We walked back to the rehab ward and found Nurse Heather, the evening-shift nurse, and Nurse Mary, with two of her daughters visiting. What luck! I had promised Shannon a reunion with nurses to get her to her appointment, and they were actually there. We also saw several therapists she had worked with. All were glad to see Shannon stronger and more talkative.

Shannon finished school and had a week off until the start of her summer program. We took her to Ocean City, New Jersey, as the beach and boardwalk provided additional stimulation. She was thrilled to run on the beach and into the waves. She managed to keep her feet straight without the DAFOs. The sandy surface of the beach required her to push off, which was a great workout. Shannon got into the building and prompt destruction of sandcastles and mocking the ever-present seagulls and their assault of beachgoer's french fries. Such activity was what I had promised Shannon she would do while she was in the coma. Living it was quite exhilarating for all of us. After cleaning up and taking a nap, Shannon got her fill of the boardwalk rides and snacks.

The next day she enjoyed the same routine accompanied by her young cousins. They were ecstatic that she was healthy this summer. Last year they had been worried after seeing her in the hospital in a wheelchair with a tube down her nose for nutrition. We were glad Shannon was enjoying normal activities. She had come so far physically, and she could also make such progress cognitively once we made that the priority.

Shannon was still having periods of agitation. At a golf course in Ocean City, she wanted no part of the holes that were constructed to resemble caves or had loud waterfalls. She would cry and simply not participate. We took her back to the hotel for a nap. We pushed her hard but backed off when necessary. Shannon was wearing down on day three. I changed things up by letting her wear the DAFOs and hold her SpongeBob kite as it flew quickly with the powerful gusts of beach wind. Shannon would be pulled along by the kite string and needed some assistance. She lost her grip a few times, forcing me to sprint and catch the kite. After a few hours, I was also tired and could not retrieve the kite in the powerful winds and current. Shannon found it hilarious and was eager to tell her mom of SpongeBob's altitude and escape.

Our next stop was the Sesame Place amusement park, about an hour's car ride from home in Pennsylvania. I was in my glory putting Shannon on my back and climbing up the cargo nets to the high slides, then holding her hand from an adjacent slide as she went down by herself. Shannon struggled to maintain trunk control on the big slides but mastered it on the smaller ones and spent lots of time cruising down, then walking up the steep but cushioned stairway. What a great workout. Sesame Place doubled as a water park, with Shannon enjoying the small waves in the wave pool and tackling the bigger ones with my assistance. Shannon enjoyed the parade and the character meet-and-greets. After six hours she was worn out, and we left.

We stopped at Cooper Trauma Center to see Nurse Pat, who was ecstatic with the visit. Pat said the whole nursing staff would refer families to Shannon's plaque when they had kids facing long odds of recovery. Shannon was very tired and not in the mood for any more activity, but what a great day. Memories like this were great because they were a healthy outlet that replaced the jarring recollection of her traumatic brain injury. Shannon also had new material from Sesame Place and Ocean City to share with her teachers and classmates. This could help with her expression and articulation skills.

The summer school program was reinforcement of the same material over a six-week period. It seemed to be more of a fun-and-games-based curriculum with lots of playground time. Shannon was still going to DuPont Hospital every Friday. PT and OT were combined in one ninety-minute group session with about ten kids and six therapists. They got the kids involved in the planning and execution process. They had to think and work together. Some of the kids did not speak, and others moved slowly. Shannon was a star in this setting with her knowledge of therapy games and familiarity with the staff's toys. Carrying water balloons over mini obstacle courses, figuring out the proper path in mini mazes, and distributing materials for arts and crafts projects were challenges the group tackled and usually accomplished. They felt like champions after the sessions and made their parents smile. During the sessions the parents would group together and discuss health insurance limitations, how to control their kids' tantrums, and any promising new programs in their school district. I usually hit the basketball courts or weight machines. All the security guards knew me by now and rarely chased me.

July 3 marked the one-year anniversary of Shannon's accident. We hosted a party with family, friends, neighbors, teachers, and some doctors and nurses who had saved Shannon, and we celebrated her recovery. The sheet cake had a picture of Shannon making another cake and holding up an icing knife. Turnout was great, and all rejoiced that Shannon was healthy and making such progress. Just like in the early days, we focused on what she was doing, not what her limitations were. Shannon was enjoying a fairly normal childhood, whereas a year ago she had not been expected to survive. She had balance issues and processing delays, and there were projections of more struggles ahead, but if we kept working, she would continue to improve. Some experts thought the brain only had one year from the date of injury to recover, but more recent research indicated the brain could continue to improve for years.

The anniversary day and moment of impact weighed heavy on my mind. It only takes a few seconds for a tragedy to occur, and the Fourth of July weekend always brings out people celebrating in reckless style. News stations always reported more drownings, accidents, and injuries on the July Fourth weekend. There is no way to guarantee safety for all. I was paranoid about people throwing firecrackers or driving while intoxicated. Chills ran up my spine all weekend as I worried about what may occur. Perhaps it was the powerful memory of Shannon on a ventilator with tubes running to and from her body and grim-faced doctors telling us that she had a very slim chance of recovering. Many family members, friends, and even neighbors recalled their difficulty in dealing with Shannon's condition and pessimistic prognosis. They reported they had sleeping troubles, stomach problems, vomiting episodes, and frequent tears.

The weekend passed incident-free for us. We caught the local fireworks show, which was impressive, but Shannon found it loud. What a contrast that was to last year. Our main medical concern was protecting her ears rather than hoping for survival in the PICU.

The neighborhood was full of young kids who rode bikes and went to the gigantic field behind the school right behind the development. They would play kickball or tag or just run around and use the mounds of dirt and trees for entertainment. Shannon would try to join in but could not keep up with the group. Most were several years older than her. Shannon was disappointed with her lack of stamina and speed. She would ask for Brian, who was enjoying the pack. I would bring the disappointed Shannon back and try to engage her with Play-Doh, arts and crafts, or T-ball. Brian would come over after his group-play activities. Shannon would get a second wind and play with Brian and his dog for hours, as she felt uplifted by his company. Shannon did not like the July and August heat and humidity. We had a small inflatable pool she would cool off in. She also loved to play with the hose and saturate me. I would become a moving target as she maintained a strong grip on the hose and extended her arms to increase the range of water. I found laughter was a great technique for dealing with her agitation. On the playground or backyard swings, I would stand in front of Shannon and fall backward when she collided with me on the downward track of the swing. This motivated her to use core strength to swing harder and strike me again.

On walks at the park, whenever Shannon was getting agitated, I would find a small grass hill and let Shannon push me down. I exaggerated the impact and tumbled down, somersaulting the next ten yards. Such activity extended outdoor play or therapy sessions. Shannon was happy to update her mom upon our return on her ability to rough me up. I did get people at the park staring and inquiring if I was OK. They asked me if I had just had a stroke, whether they should call 911. Clearly they thought I was nuts, but I did not care, as I had an opportunity to help my daughter recover and was not going to hold back.

Shannon attended some neighborhood birthday parties and joined right in with the activities. At one pool party, she could not keep up with the kids jumping in the water over and over. She found a dog outside and came up with a leash and walked him around the house. After an hour she was worn out, so we left for a brief nap. She returned wearing her DAFOs and resumed walking the dog in time for the cake and ice cream. Some of the kids had questions, and I responded with short statements about how great she was doing.

Rain or triple-digit temperatures did curtail outdoor activities. Fortunately the playroom was chock-full of games we had acquired over the past year. Most of them had motor skill applications. Games like Trouble and Don't Wake Daddy required manipulation with hands, which worked Shannon's fine motor skills. She still had ataxia, which was not noticeable to most but was clear when she tried to string beads together. Play-Doh was the most popular activity for fine motor skills, as Shannon would make fruits and vegetables and laugh at the results.

At times all games failed, and we had to improvise. Shannon enjoyed ripping up tissues and throwing them in the air and saying, "It's snowing." What an upbeat use of tissues, compared to the boxes we went through when she was in intensive care. She also would color on anything, up to and including the walls. I could usually wipe off the art with the help of WD-40 but did have to slap paint on once in a while. Jan had to have noticed, but she did not complain, as she knew I was keeping Shannon on the move and chasing her agitation.

There was an ice hockey rink up the street that became a weekly destination. There were games or practice all day long with toddlers to adults hitting the ice. Shannon and I would watch slick skaters and newcomers alike, and she would comment on their proficiency. It was cold and damp, but Shannon came up with hilarious comments on every visit such as, "PT Monica could help that guy" (when a player struggled to maintain balance on skates), "He needs Nurse Mary" (when a player was injured), and "It's freezing; get me some french fries." The snack bar was heated and right next to an arcade that had games full of lights and bells. Shannon started to ask to go to the rink, which was right next to the library. That combination made it a very constructive outing. The library, with its vast selection of books, became another frequent destination. We would read a few books; walk around the library, as Shannon loved to locate and drink from water fountains; and then read a few more books. The pet store was another resource, with the cats, birds, fish, and friendly staff.

When all recreational activity failed, we resorted to short drives in the car with a destination like McDonald's. The Barney music in the car usually calmed her down, and the McDonald's chicken nuggets and ice cream sundae desserts filled her up.

On a couple of rare occasions, I had nothing left to keep Shannon entertained. Jan would step in and take her to the mall. I was encouraged one day when Shannon returned with two water pistols from the toy store, stating, "Look what I found at the mall. One for me, one for Brian." That was clear evidence Shannon's mind was working in regard to planning and following up. She also frequently returned with Barbie-themed toys to expand her Barbie empire.

Shannon's comments also reflected an ability to compare and contrast. One day she surprised me by saying, "You don't have mermaid hair like me; you have short hair like Caillou." Thirteen words of accuracy! I was impressed. Caillou was a four-year-old on PBS who described his daily adventures. He was nearly bald like I was, since I had lost all my remaining hair from the stress of the realities of Shannon's traumatic brain injury. Such recognition and commentary were significant signs of brain systems working together. All STs would be impressed.

The next day Shannon asked for an orange. I asked her if she wanted it now or later. Her reply floored me. "Right now, with no hesitation whatsoever." "With no hesitation whatsoever" was one of my favorite phrases. Shannon recognized this and used it as appropriately as possible! Bad weather made it harder to calm Shannon when she became agitated. One day I saw a commercial for the new Tropicana casino in Atlantic City that described an indoor mall in an outdoor setting that resembled cafés in Havana, Cuba. We rolled there with no hesitation whatsoever and found the stores and restaurants set in the casino hotel with a ceiling that replicated blue sky and clouds. Palm trees, gigantic Cuban fans, and torch lighting reinforced a tropical setting. There were stores with expensive clothing and modern electronic gadgets for sale along with fancy restaurants and specialty stores for pet treats and decorations. Shannon was energized by the setting and got a workout from checking everything out. Most casino visitors just transited the mall to get from the hotel to the gaming area, which made it less crowded. Just fifty miles from our house, we found an outlet that was a real escape from the downpours that continued for hours. The Tropicana turned into an enjoyable outing, which was what the family needed.

Shannon and her dad enjoying steep slides

16

PRESSURE TO MAINSTREAM

Shannon returned to her preschool program and continued to make slow but steady progress. We met with the child study team several times, and they recommended Shannon attend the full-day kindergarten program in the fall of 2002. Most kids attended the half-day program. The full-day program was for students that had some type of disability. The class had about ten students with a special education teacher, her assistant, and several aides for students. The kids all appeared to be healthy learners but had struggles with attention deficit disorder, hyperactive conditions, or other learning or speech challenges. Shannon had a one-to-one aide. As she grew stronger throughout the year, she did not need as much help in getting around. The aide did have to frequently refocus the distracted Shannon on the task at hand. I still fielded frequent questions from many people on how Shannon was doing.

I always gave glowing reports on her progress and recall mentioning we were trying to determine if she was ready for the regular kindergarten or the specialized all-day version. Most would respond that we should put her in the regular class. Some would ask why we wanted her stuck in a self-contained class, especially in the simple setting of kindergarten, where all that was taught was simple things like colors and numbers. I knew all hoped for the best, but I had to make sure Shannon was placed in the best setting. In the mainstreamed classroom, there was a risk Shannon would fall behind. The all-day version had the special education teacher and more staffing to meet Shannon's needs. We went with the all-day version, as we were pleased with the teacher's commitments and her multisensory approach to learning.

The class had eight boys and two girls. I recalled reading that learning-disabled boys outnumbered girls five to one. This held true, and some of the boys were jumpy, to say the least. Shannon blended in fine in the rough-and-tumble class. Each night we drilled on the letters, numbers, words, and concepts.

Over the summer, We were still making trips to DuPont every Friday. Shannon would sleep on the way down. She would change and have breakfast at the Ronald McDonald House of Delaware and work hard in the three-hour therapy sessions. Monica the PT was the only continuing therapist, and she had been out a few months on maternity leave. The turnover rate was high. Nurse Mary was still there but informed us of several other nurses departing to other locations. Even the health-care industry has lots of turnover. All remaining staff members were happy with Shannon's progress. She loved seeing her friends on the staff and checking on young patients, especially the babies. We would frequently run into nurses and therapists who had cared for Shannon occasionally. I doubted that Shannon could remember all, but she would walk, talk, and proudly display her outfit for the shocked staff members. They would start tearing up at the results of Shannon's recovery, which they had played a part in.

Parents of other patients with traumatic brain injury seemed to know of Shannon and inquired about how she had been able to rapidly recover. I answered that the reason was the great care and therapy here at DuPont and the continuing stimulation at home, as much as she could tolerate. I told them to focus on what their child was doing as opposed to what they were not doing. This approach had worked for me, but I questioned how sound this advice was, as some kids were doing very little. The parents looked run down and overwhelmed by the struggle. Some asked how I could always be with Shannon at DuPont instead of working. I explained shift work and accumulated leave. It felt good to be a reference point for the other families, as traumatic brain injury is an arduous journey with few bright spots for most.

Toward the end of 2002, Shannon had progressed enough to scale back her checkups with Dr. Ray to every six months. A medical student on internship would evaluate Shannon first and find some delays in her reflexes and ataxia in her limbs. Dr. Ray would then check Shannon and show other physical deficiencies with gross or fine motor skills. The medical student seemed surprised in all cases. At first, I was not thrilled Shannon was being used as a training case. Dr. Ray once said to the medical student and to me, "This is why we are treating the new patient in room 12A. Shannon's insurance companies pushed me not to treat her but to send her to a long-term care facility so the funds would last longer. I knew there was a lot of little girl in Shannon, and she would respond."

I felt grateful Dr. Ray had been determined to help Shannon from the jump and was OK with him using Shannon's case to educate his students. They would be faced with the same tough battles ahead. Dr. Ray would continue by watching Shannon walk up and down the hallway, then run, then attempt to hop on each foot. Shannon displayed improvement on each visit but could barely hop on her left foot and not at all on her right foot. Dr. Ray was overjoyed with her progress and encouraged us to keep up the exercise routines and cognitive activities.

Checkups with Dr. Ray were in the main part of the hospital, which was a high-traffic area. We would occasionally run into specialists who had treated Shannon. We always recognized the doctors before they recognized us. They struggled to make the connection between the healthy Shannon and the critically ill Shannon from July 2000. The pediatric attending physician in the rehab wing said she had seen Shannon's plaque at the Ronald McDonald House of Delaware and had broken into tears. The orthopedic surgeon that treated her broken wrist was shocked upon being told this was Shannon. He was the one expert in the early days at DuPont who'd said a remarkable recovery was possible after the brain swelling went down. He referred to Shannon as "the girl that pulled her hand out of a cast." The girls in the casting room remembered Shannon and celebrated the straightness of her feet.

Recoveries like Shannon's were rare. We were glad she was getting recognition, which made her feel good and the staff feel better. Even with Shannon's progress, I still received a mailbox full of medical bills. Car insurance and health insurance covered most expenses but not all. The bills piled up as I had my brother Barry speak to both companies on a regular basis. Shannon's recovery was organized, but nothing else was. I had spent no time working on the house, so items needing attention accumulated. All my time was spent working with Shannon or working, so Jan and I spent almost no time together, something not good for any marriage. My window of opportunity for Shannon's recovery was limited, so what choice did I have but to give all my time and efforts to her and hope for the best in everything else? I did maintain the intensity on my job with US Customs. Some asked why I worked so diligently when I had off-duty challenges and was with an agency that would never appreciate my efforts. I found that when I was busiest on the job, I got the best ideas for new therapeutic activities with Shannon. Many coworkers chose the path of least resistance and stood around avoiding work, then justified their approach with monologues that slammed management and the union. These guys had no medical or financial challenges and chose to complain lots and do little. I was grateful I had the energy to drive on and hoped better days were ahead.

Shannon loved her day-long kindergarten program. The teacher and her aides were extremely dedicated and had all kinds of strategies to reinforce learning concepts. It was a five-day program, which meant Shannon would not be attending DuPont for anything beyond medical checkups. Nurse Mary was now an instructor to brand-new nurses. PT Monica and OT Sandra were working part time with new babies at home. DuPont's rehab team had a farewell party for Shannon with lots of comments of how far she had come, how her personality and fashion sense would be missed, how her classy mom had made an impact, and how her crazy dad would do anything to help the recovery process. Shannon promised to visit everyone when on her quarterly checkups concurrent with her stops at the Ronald McDonald House of Delaware. She proudly walked out of the hospital with positive memories and celebrity status.

Shannon had no recollection of the accident or her early days in painful rehab sessions. We felt better that such an injury erased short-term memory. Shannon would remember this as an experience. We would never forget it as a living nightmare. DuPont Hospital and the Ronald McDonald House of Delaware were full of professionals who helped us overcome the harrowing demons of traumatic brain injury.

The full days of schoolwork and Shannon's continued progress reduced my daily workouts with Shannon to four hours, which enabled me to maintain a constant work schedule most of the time. I remained a productive employee, but my thoughts were still dominated by Shannon's recovery process.

One day Senator Joe Biden of Delaware arrived at the airport traveling from Afghanistan with only one security specialist. I reached out to him, knowing his wife, Jill, was on the board of directors at the Ronald McDonald House of Delaware. I was surprised when he replied, "Call me Joe" to my greeting of "Senator Biden." We discussed the greatness of DuPont Hospital. I showed him a picture of Shannon, and he said he had seen her plaque on the wall on a recent visit to the house and was aware of her recovery. Senator Biden shared with me the story of his family being in a car accident that his wife and daughter did not survive and in which his young sons were severely injured (one with a brain injury). His sons made remarkable recoveries and did well in school.

After he left, my colleagues asked if I had inquired about higher salaries and better benefits for federal workers. I answered, "No. We talked about DuPont Hospital and brain injuries." They looked at me like I was kidding. Amazing how the health of your family becomes so important that all other issues pale in comparison. Here I was in front of a powerful senator who was on lots of committees and whom my agency directors and national union leaders would love to talk to, and we did not even visit the pay, compensations, or agency role topics. It was very unusual to see a senator or congressman traveling without at least a few advance or support personnel, and the fact that Senator Biden did not showed what an unassuming person he was. December provided more decorated stores to visit and an invitation to the Ronald McDonald House of Delaware's Share a Night Ceremony. Thousands of people bought lights at fifteen dollars each, and these lights covered every inch of the house. The donations went to pay for a night at the house for a family that could not afford the fifteen-dollar fee. There was a full program of holiday carols, a magic show by Ronald McDonald, and speeches by major donors and a family that was staying at the house. They were short speeches. I was so glad they did not ask me that year.

All would go outside and count down, and then an ill child would join Ronald to flick the main switch; the illumination was magnificent. We would recognize many people and hear of many new cases of brain injury with families struggling to deal with all the life-changing issues. Shannon was in her glory but hoping to find Kirby in the crowd. Kirby's handlers wisely kept him home. I was determined to stay active with the house, as Shannon was a great inspiration to all, and she brought a jolt of happiness to the staff.

I bought an interactive Elmo-based computer game and taught Shannon the basics of using the mouse to move the object to Elmo. He would commend correct choices and give more details on mistakes. After a week of me helping Shannon, she could play the game herself. Shannon would say, "Dad, go watch football or do sit-ups; I can do it myself." Her cognitive skills clearly had come a long way. Once several sections were mastered, Elmo got a birthday cake and an on-screen celebration.

Shannon would also ask questions or make suggestions indicating she was alert. I took her with me to Jiffy Lube, and Shannon wanted details. "Dad, what is oil? Why does the car need oil?" Additional examples of Shannon's comments reflecting that the executive portion of her brain was working:

- "Dad, you need gas. It's empty. Dad, get gas."
- "Dad, let's go back to the pet store; they let the dogs in to walk around at nighttime."
- "Dad, the toy store is near the pet store. Let's get more Play-Doh so we don't run out and have to get the small cans from CVS."
- "Dad, Joe and Mike keep arguing on the bus. Can you make them laugh again so they calm down?"
- "Dad, let me see if we have any food for you." [Opens the fridge, then closes it]. "Nope, we have to go shopping for snacks."
- "Dad, I got two mosquito bites on my leg. Mom had to put cream on them. I am going to the mall now. You have to cut the grass when you get back to chase the mosquitoes away."

Shannon in her glory on a Friday session at DuPont Hospital.

17

SHANNON SLUGS MORE HEARTS AWAY

Every parent dreams of their child participating in organized sports and doing well in the interaction and competition. Shannon was as knowledgeable about baseball as any five-year-old girl. She would join me watching Phillies games, and during our workouts at the park, we frequently stopped to watch Little League or adult softball games. I signed her up for T-ball in the spring and hoped she would get a coach who would not let her balance and coordination issues be a burden.

Shannon was assigned to Coach Ted's team, and he was joined by a group of assistants from his neighborhood. They brought great enthusiasm with them and coached in a way five-year-olds would understand. For example, they told the girls to "open the alligator's mouth" when fielding grounders and to "hold the bow and arrow" when standing to throw the ball. Shannon actually had an advantage in hitting, as she had been hitting off the tee in dozens of therapy sessions and knew how to hold her arms back, elbow up, swing level, and follow through with the bat. Coach Ted and his assistants tweaked her swing, and she could drive the ball as well as anyone.

We got Shannon baseball cleats and got used to putting them on over her DAFOs. She picked out her own glove and got lots of repetition practice through catching tennis balls. Shannon could quickly make contact with the ball on the tee and start running to first base. Shannon's run was more of a sideways hop with her right side lagging behind. All the girls were learning the game with few understanding the rules of running the bases. Some were very distracted and chased butterflies or pulled dandelions in the outfield. No one was very proficient in defense. All the girls would make contact with the bat, then run to first base, with most throws arriving late and off-target. Shannon regularly made contact on her first swing and hit a slower ground ball to an infielder, which gave her more time to beat any throw.

After ten batters all hit singles, they switched sides. Shannon was slower to react on defense, so the coaches kept her to the second base, shortstop, or outfield positions. She loved to get the ball and throw it and learned to stick with the ball as she would knock it down, then get the deflected ball, then wind up and throw. Shannon's experience at hitting off the tee gave her the opportunity to reach out to teammates. Some of the girls struggled, and Shannon was happy to assist. Early in the season, she would reach out to teammates with advice. "My dad taught me how to hit baseballs in the backyard. Hold it like this. Stand this way. Get arms back and elbow up. Line it up, then watch the ball and swing hard, and the ball takes off." What a description! Shannon explained and demonstrated the art of T-ball, using several parts of her brain in conjunction to remember the technique, demonstrate it, and explain it to peers!

She was gaining social skills through baseball, which was great as her classes were full of boys but this team was all girls. The last batter every half inning got the opportunity to circle the bases after hitting her grounder and was given credit for a home run. Shannon had several such home runs and was proud of her contributions. Seeing her run the bases with a wide grin was a spectacular realization of the dreams we had had at DuPont Hospital.

Shannon's favorite moments were right after the game, when snacks were distributed. She looked forward to her turn for the snacks and planned out getting her favorite items. Shannon enjoyed the interaction and had regular discussions on the bench, which served as the dugout. She loved the cheering the girls did for one another and the constant compliment of "Nice hit." All the girls earned a participation trophy, and I will never forget Shannon's grin upon getting her trophy from Coach Ted. I usually took a few hours of leave to catch Shannon's game when I was on a later shift, as I was not going to miss this happiness.

Some of the parents knew of Shannon's journey, but many did not. All gave her enormous support as the results were remarkable, heartwarming, and a chunk of the normalcy we had been hoping for.

One evening after a successful game, we got Shannon to bed early. Jan surprised me with the news that she was pregnant! What a continuation of positive developments. First Shannon was playing organized sports with her peers, then I found out our family would be growing. I was pleasantly surprised, as we were hoping for more children, but all our recent efforts had gone toward Shannon's recovery. Jan's doctor had told her he doubted she would get pregnant again after she had had some medical issues. Jan expressed thoughts that perhaps the baby would be a boy and join me in lots of guy activities. All I really hoped for was a healthy child. Shannon was glad to welcome a sibling and made all sorts of plans for shifting her toys from Barbie dolls to things boys would also enjoy.

On May 17, 2002, we went for the eight-month checkup, with Jan looking ready to deliver any minute. Tests showed signs of preeclampsia, so we rushed to the hospital and were told the baby was to be delivered that night. Shannon was overjoyed with the early arrival and told the doctors to take care of her mom and brother. I raced home and left Shannon with her niece, then raced back to the hospital and made it just in time for my son's birth via C-section. He was a healthy six pounds, so there were no complications despite his being delivered at eight months.

The next day Shannon and I stopped for balloons and flowers and went to the hospital to see her brother, whom we named Tim. She was in her glory with discussions with the nursing staff and proudly introducing Timmy to all visitors. This birth was easier for Jan, as Shannon had been an emergency C-section after twelve hours of labor. We were glad for our expanding family and happy Shannon had a companion to interact with. Shannon told Tim she would take him to school on show-and-tell day, introduce him to our cat, and show him all the Disney movies. Such planning was a great sign of the executive part of the brain working.

Late that summer we enrolled Shannon in a soccer league for five-year-olds. It included boys and girls on a tiny field. Getting Shannon's soccer shoes on over the DAFOs was still a challenge. Unlike baseball, soccer has collisions and contact, and I might have been taking a risk. I explained my concerns to the coach, who said that all the kids were lacking skills and some just stood around while others watched birds and clouds. Shannon got in great workouts during practices, which tested her stamina. When the kids were told to run a lap, Shannon fell way behind, but a coach accompanied her to completion. In the games Shannon understood the concept and stuck with the clump of kids chasing the ball. She managed a few assists over the season but was late to arrive at the developing plays.

Just as in the T-ball season, Shannon's favorite part was snack time after the games. Shannon became close friends with one of the girls on the team. The end-of-season pizza party and participation trophy was another high point for us. The highlight of the year was definitely the first game, when Jan, six-month-old Tim, and I watched Shannon as she ran by us and yelled in her raspy voice with vocal cord paralysis, "Mom, Dad, Tim, I am doing it. I am playing soccer."

Shannon drives the ball with confidence at her T-ball game

18

MAXIMIZING THE MOVEMENT

Shannon's therapists made a point to get her doing things with both hands. It was helpful in getting the hemispheres of the brain to work together and overcoming balance and coordination issues. Such movement should also help her to focus, so I started looking for a dance studio and karate school, as both disciplines required movement to a memorized routine. There were many studios in the area, but I needed one that understood Shannon's recovery process and had the patience to work with her. I found a smaller studio with an experienced instructor named Miss Jill. She had a program for four- and five-year-olds. Shannon showed no hesitation whatsoever in blending in with the toddlers twirling to her favorite Disney classics. She did not wear the DAFOs during dance class. She only wore the soft dance shoes and was noticeably wobbly in the studio setting.

Miss Jill kept her focused and making progress. She would slow things down when the girls got tired and kept them laughing and learning. Miss Jill also agreed to work with Shannon on private lessons to really develop her balance and coordination. Shannon's lack of focus stood out more in the private lessons. Miss Jill had to repeat instructions and provide hand support for Shannon to complete the turns and spins. In a matter of a few weeks, she was hooked on Shannon and determined to help her improve. This was a great form of PT and the perfect transition away from the expensive professional sessions at DuPont.

Shannon attended one group class and one private lesson a week. I hoped this routine would help her cognitive focus as well. Movement is the best thing to help the mind to focus. A local karate studio also had a program for three- to five-year-olds that was strictly no contact. We jumped on the six-weeks-for-ninety-nine-dollars special. Shannon wore the traditional loose shirt and pants and white belt and took to the mat with her normal enthusiasm. She pretended she was Mulan from Disney and learned basic punches and a few kicks that she rarely finished in the standing position. The sensei were great with the kids, as they flipped backward upon absorbing the kids' strikes. The class consisted of warm-ups, basic kata movements, classroom instruction on dedication or focus, a run through a simple obstacle course, and dodgeball. Dodgeball scared me, as some kids were over the top. I made the sensei shadow Shannon so she would not get run over. The ball was of soft Nerf material so was safe.

All this back and forth to dance or karate class was time consuming, but we were convinced that it was a more challenging form of therapy than the daily drills she got at home. She also enjoyed the interaction with peers, and it was something to look forward to besides school and trips to DuPont or the Ronald McDonald House of Delaware. It was returning some normalcy to Shannon's world. Jan or I would run her to the classes and sit with the other parents. As usual Jan would engage in conversation while I would read books or articles on brain injury.

The books were heavy reading at times, but they provided lots of complex science on brain function and slow recovery when injured. I started to notice a theme that frequent movement involving all limbs was key to recovery and was glad Shannon's therapists had always advocated and implemented such movement into her sessions. I made continuing this practice a priority.

There were days when Shannon was tired and would not go to karate or dance class. We would arrive at karate, and Shannon would say, "Take me back to dance class." At times she would say she had quit karate or dance, but the next day she would say she was only kidding. Once she said it was an April Fools' joke. Dance class was hard on her legs, especially after a day of school. Karate was usually more entertaining, depending on who the instructor was. She stuck with both but did not participate in the karate tournaments. She may have recognized she was slower than her peers and that competition would be frustrating. We did not force her to participate when she was worn out. We redirected her to her arts and crafts or home-work or writing letters consisting of short words. Shannon was accustomed to all this activity and not the type to entertain herself.

When I was at work on weekends and she was home, she could test the patience of her mom and visitors by expecting entertaining activities. She started to call me at work with ten-minute updates on her own therapeutic activities. She would start with the location and activity of her cat, brief me on whether Mom was busy cleaning and not available to take her out, and ask what she should try next. I would suggest games like hiding her Barbie dolls or stuffed animals, which would make her think and follow up. She could turn on the computer, start her favorite games, operate the VCR or DVD player, and go through her vast collection of arts and crafts activities. When I got home, she usually had suggestions for outings like the park, pet store, bookstore, or mall after I recovered her concealed toys. I would struggle in my search, forcing her to provide clues.

A neurological psychologist at DuPont had told us to get Shannon planning and acting on plans to get multiple systems of her brain working together. I finally had a few hours of downtime and tackled some home-im-provement projects. The back deck needed new floorboards. The old ones were easy to yank out, but the new ones took longer to install than expected. Shannon was eager to join me and enjoyed hammering nails in. I would get them started, and Shannon would follow through. Her aim was frequently off and her power limited, but she got plenty of shots in and enjoyed the results. Next was a chain-link fence to replace the old wooden one. Shannon helped with digging holes for the poles but quickly had enough. Another project was washing the aluminum siding, which was her favorite task. Shannon held the hose with two hands and fired away. When her arms got tired, she redirected the stream to the bushes and plants. Shannon was proud of her contributions and had new experiences to tell people about.

Shannon continued to do well on her occasional visits to DuPont and the Ronald McDonald House of Delaware. She was happy to introduce all to her brother and give details of her job getting the diaper and baby powder whenever required. The staff of the Ronald McDonald House of Delaware was ecstatic, expressing that we had proven the doctors wrong several times now. They also said they had heard details of my recent speech to the United Way group and found it very powerful. I had given my normal spiel on the mission of the house and how it benefited us and so many other families of critically injured children. We did feel a sense of accomplishment at having found some success when confronted with complex medical challenges.

Back to Shannon, who was testing at the skill level of a four-year-old in some areas. Who would have thought this was possible? Her voice continued to grow stronger but still was raspy from the vocal cord paralysis. The dance lessons continued, with Shannon showing steady improvement. Dance class was a great bargain compared to the expensive PT sessions. It was also a social outing, with Shannon connecting with other girls on the dance steps and fashion opportunities. Shannon even graduated from DAFOs on both feet to a MAFO (molded ankle foot orthosis) on her left foot, which provided support on the foot only and did not extend up the calf. She was nearing the same status on her right foot. The MAFOs would keep her feet straight, and they were not very noticeable. Shannon's PT at school did not agree with this decision, but DuPont and Dr. Ray were on board, and they knew best. Clearly the dance sessions with Miss Jill paid off. We had been told Shannon would need the DAFOs the rest of her life, but such progress was encouraging. At this rate she could not need any such orthopedic support in a few years. How could I ever repay the debt to my sister Anne, who'd ranged Shannon's feet every day when she was in a coma, was so instrumental in the move to DuPont, and helped us with complicated decisions like injecting Shannon's calves with non-FDA-approved Botox?

Anne was presented with the Mercy Courage Award from her employer, Mercy FitzGerald Hospital, for her work with patients with life-threatening injuries. The award recognized her for providing all patients with comprehensive rehabilitation care and the understanding and compassion they needed to reach their full potential. The brochure continued to describe how Anne motivated and challenged her patients not to give up hope and not to give in to their disabilities. As unlucky as Shannon was to get struck by a vehicle, she had benefited from having an aunt who was a world-class PT by her side.

Anne's guidance included keeping Shannon active in pools, as the resistance coupled with the water's buoyancy would strengthen a muscle group. I wanted to keep her active in swimming, but the closest YMCA was seven miles away. Pool technology had come a long way, and smaller versions could be found for one hundred dollars. I found one that was twelve-by-sixteen inches with plastic piping that supported a vinyl frame; a small but proficient pump kept the water clean. Assembly was easy, and bags of shock, chlorine, and antialgae chemicals had it sparkling clear. Shannon and her friend Brian enjoyed it as Shannon remembered a routine she had learned from Monica in aquatic therapy. Shannon got lots of work on core strength while cooling off and worked on floating and basic strokes. I hoped she would outgrow it in a few years so I could get a more challenging pool despite the expense.

Shannon still dealt with bouts of agitation several times a week. It usually hit later in the day, when she was tired. I would back off of any activity and let her relax. Other times she needed a trip to a pet store or some destination where she could throw rocks in the water or see something different. One day I was fried from burning the candle at both ends and only had the energy to go around the corner to CVS. CVS had a fine selection of cards for all occasions; Shannon pulled the humorous ones and showed me the characters.

We ran into Shannon's PT from school, who gave me a glorious report on Shannon's balance, walking, and focus, adding that her ataxia and forefoot abduction were less prevalent. She asked where I got the strength to work with Shannon on a daily basis while dealing with the struggle of having a healthy daughter being so seriously injured and the enormous impact that has on life. She encouraged me to keep pushing the school district, as we were seeing results, and such persistent parents were rare. Shannon sought the attention and started telling me to find a clock by yelling, "Ticktock, ticktock." The PT said it was easy to keep Shannon engaged and that she was not seeing the zoning-out problem that the classroom teachers were. It was great to hear the refreshing news from a member of Shannon's team at the school.

Perhaps if we kept Shannon moving in class, she would stay alert. I made a mental note to email the teachers with this info. Shannon would grow frustrated when things didn't go as planned. Our computer would frequently freeze, and I could reset or manipulate it when home but not when at work. Shannon would call me complaining the computer did not work or the rain wouldn't stop. I tried to talk her on to another activity, but this was not easy over the phone. She would tear apart her playroom in search of a certain toy.

Shannon tested the patience of her mom and a visiting cousin who was staying with us. She had such high levels of energy, which was an asset most of the time but hard to control when agitation struck. Agitation could be a challenge, but we focused on all she was doing that experts said would not happen. An easy solution would be to resort to medication to help her focus and reduce agitation. Such medicine had side effects, so we chose not to resort to that. Shannon stuck with watching Disney movies, and her new favorites were *Cinderella II* and *Mulan*. I found a Sesame Street movie called *Elmocize* that had Elmo and his friends trying to get people to exercise. They would do all sorts of aerobics and encourage people, including a cranky old man named Mr. Martin, to get active. Shannon joined right in and followed the Muppets' lead in thirty minutes of exercise. *Elmocize* became a frequently watched video. Even Shannon's leisure time was interupted with movement drills.

Shannon eagerly accepted her brother's arrival

19

FIRST-GRADE HIGHS AND LOWS

In 2003 Shannon transitioned to an inclusive first-grade program that had her spending half the day in a small class for reading, math, and English and half the day in the main class for gym, art, history, and science. She had a one-on-one aide to keep her focused in class. Her kindergarten teacher had pushed for a self-contained-type setting due to Shannon's frequent daydreaming and lack of focus, but the rest of the group had thought she could keep up. This in-class support setting in which a second teacher in the class stuck with the students in the smaller classes was a new format that many schools were migrating to.

Both of Shannon's first-grade teachers were very sharp and committed. After the first gym class, we got a call from an alarmed physical education teacher who needed an immediate meeting to get our approval to remove Shannon from the main gym class for safety reasons. I explained to her Shannon's successful participation in T-ball and soccer and her relentless work ethic to overcome any challenge. They agreed to leave Shannon in the main gym class with her aide intervening in any activities that would be too much of a struggle for her. I had the school PT, who had worked with Shannon in the early-intervention setting and kindergarten, on my side.

Shannon did fairly well the first few months of first grade, then began to struggle as the class sped up the pace. We were called in for another meeting in which the teacher gave examples of Shannon not grasping necessary concepts. I wondered if I should have listened to the kindergarten teacher who'd recommended the smaller classroom with more support. We agreed to keep Shannon in a summer program to catch up and planned on moving her the next year to the self-contained class, where two teachers taught twelve first-, second-, and third-graders the basic skills.

Shannon's T-ball and soccer successes were not being duplicated in the classroom. Teachers said she would raise her hand and comment completely off-topic. This was something else I had come across in my readings. It was called confabulation and resulted from the right and left hemispheres of the brain not working together and filling in the memory gaps with other material. As I mentioned in pervious chapters, Shannon's therapists encouraged us to have Shannon doing as many activities as possible using both arms at the same time to get both hemispheres of her brain working together. I committed Shannon to a year's worth of karate classes, as that would help this problem, and planned on dropping the soccer to replace it with cheerleading in the fall.

Math class was by far Shannon's biggest struggle. She still confused threes with eights and twos with fives, perhaps because they look very similar. Her aide would walk her through the steps and provide the answer hoping Shannon would catch on, but it was a real struggle. I also recalled reading that the part of the brain that processed math was the same part that dealt with music. I started playing music constantly during math homework and trying to get Shannon to pick up music notes on a toy keyboard. Shannon generally responded well to the constant stream of stimulation. She would get tired and frustrated at times, and we gave her the necessary breaks. She was definitely overscheduled with dance class, karate class, T-ball, and soccer, plus hours of reinforcement on topics covered in school in addition to daily work on balance. What six-year-old could endure such a schedule, but what choice did we have as progress now would enable her to do well in the future and avoid frustration?

I started to understand how some parents took paths of less resistance and accepted the blows fate had dealt their children. It was quite exhausting to run her around every day. Between work and Shannon's activities, we had little time as a family, which was not good. Coworkers would talk about TV programs and current events that I was unaware of. I spent time with Tim, but most of it was bringing him to watch Shannon's activities. He was a great partner, with the other moms fussing over him and with his frequent participation in the activities. Tim could find friends in minutes as a one-year-old. He blended right in with the siblings of Shannon's peers. They would usually find an adjacent field or playground and start some interactive game.

One of my favorite memories of Tim was when he took charge of a group of peers, all one or two years old, as they watched Shannon's karate class from the seating area designated for parents. He was wearing his Eagles quarterback Donovan McNabb jersey and ready for Monday Night Football amid the Eagles Super Bowl season of 2004. They were making so much noise that the sensei suggested the kids move to the other mat room, which was not being used. Tim led the charge into the room, where the toddlers found unused inflated strike bags. They proceeded to pound them and celebrate each participant's strike with applause and loud cheers. The annoyed sensei made us parents break up the pep rally. Tim had somehow let them know there was an Eagles game in a few hours. Some of them mumbled, "Let's go, Eagles" or "Big game tonight" as we pulled them out of the room and tried to get them to settle down. On our next visit to the karate studio, there was a new sign in big bold letters that said, "Please control your children when class is in session. Any vacant mat room is off-limits." Tim did not like this restriction. I usually managed to redirect him and his mates with blocks or LEGOs.

Most kids with attention issues are on medication. I had considered this option in great detail and decided not to use any stimulants. They held the potential to help in the short term, but research had proven exercise programs were more effective. The stimulants had side effects we were not willing to risk. Shannon had taken all sorts of medication while hospitalized and was on the antiseizure medication Tegretol for an entire year, which is what caused the car sickness en route to DuPont Hospital. We did not want her dependent on medication that had no guarantee of working and had side effects.

Shannon attended some of her cousins' high school graduation parties and came up with the idea of hosting her own party to celebrate her graduation from first grade. She invited the entire class and planned a menu of pizza, hot dogs, and mac and cheese. She told all to bring their bathing suits, and all twenty-two students complied and enjoyed the matchbox-size pool. They played rough games full of collisions that had the water splashing out and kids colliding in the middle. I was sure the pool would collapse, as the frame was shaking and sides twisting, but it stayed together. All the kids had a blast, and Shannon gained a powerful memory of her first-grade graduation.

Later that summer I took Shannon to the Ocean City beach one day, and we attended a beach event hosted by the New Jersey Brain Injury Association. I'd had some previous contact with them to inquire about any additional resources available that we could use. They were impressed with Shannon's array of therapies and transition to the school system and said they were trying to help other families get such services. We were not prepared for what we would see. There were over a thousand people at the event. Several hundred were brain injury victims, and each one seemed to have several family-member caregivers. Most were using beach wheelchairs with large rubber wheels. The family members were positioning the wheelchairs in the surf and splashing the ocean water onto their loved ones. Many victims could not move their limbs to the water or react upon feeling the water. Other victims were healthier in appearance but yelling inappropriate comments and were under the close watch of caregivers. Some victims were in stretchers and were only capable of being in the salt air and sun. This event truly impressed on me how far Shannon had come. Everyone we saw was no younger than twenty years of age, so clearly the brain's ability to recover is greater in kids than adults.

Karate and dance lessons continued through the summer, but we decided to try cheerleading in the fall. Cheerleading was another activity that combined movement of arms and legs. It also required vocalization of memorized cheers and expressing oneself with enthusiasm and style. Practice started in late August, so Shannon had to deal with the heat and sun. Cheerleading had over twenty girls and was run by committed moms who kept the girls busy. Shannon loved the drama of games, the outfit changes each month as the weather got colder, and the new friends she made. Her movement was a step slower than that of the rest of the unit but not very noticeable from the sidelines. Shannon memorized the cheers and had a good season. She hated the cold and wind and had had enough after one season. She had had another positive experience that was beneficial physically, cognitively, and socially. I frequently took Tim to her practice and games. The moms adored him, and he loved the attention.

Shannon proud to collect recognition from her cheerleading squad

20

TWO ANGELS TAKE CHARGE OF

TEACHING SECOND GRADE

Shannon started second grade in 2004 in the smaller class that combined first-, second-, and third-grade students with two teachers and several aides. I had visited the class toward the end of first grade and been impressed. Mrs. Collin and Mrs. C were experienced, organized, enthusiastic, and of the same quality of professionalism as Nurse Pat at Cooper and Nurse Mary at DuPont. They convinced all their students to participate with such enthusiasm, and that had to be the product of decades of experience.

Their approach included dancing before academics, jobs for all students, weekly and monthly recognition for deserving students, holiday-themed art activities, cooking banana bread or other treats, and raising caterpillars to butterflies in class. There was a lot of parental involvement in the class as the two instructors encouraged students to try new things. The teachers hosted class meetings to resolve conflicts between students and had older students familiarize younger ones with daily procedures and end-of-year shows. They used the multisensory form of learning that was common in kindergarten but less so in the first grade.

They had the list of goals from Shannon's IEP, and they unofficially added the main goal of getting Shannon to be more independent. They had her one-to-one aide monitor things but not get directly involved unless Shannon's agitation surfaced. By the middle of the year, they had changed Shannon's aide status from one-to-one to a shared aide with the concurrence of the learning specialist, guidance counselor, and PT. By the end of the year, they recommended that Shannon not have an aide the following year in third grade. Talk about results!

How did they accomplish this? Some of the jobs required students to walk to the main office or cafeteria with information like attendance figures or lunch orders. They sent Shannon out with the data and no aide. The aide would shadow from a distance and only engage if necessary. Shannon developed the confidence to handle more-challenging tasks. We thought Shannon was exaggerating with her reports of walking to the cafeteria to turn in data showing how many classmates would be purchasing lunch, but she was accurately describing her task and results. Mrs. Collin described Shannon as "like sunshine." She said she was very popular and would let her walk around at times to visit friends and last year's teachers in school.

The smaller groups helped as with three grades in one class, there was constant small-group work. Shannon did not comment off-topic in class, which had been a problem in first grade. They did notice her zoning out but would redirect her immediately. They would also hold her responsible for completing tasks and following directions through a form of quiet leadership that motivated all to work hard. Mrs. Collin had two rules: try your best and support each other. This seemed to take the competition out of the classroom and remove the struggle that sometimes accompanies it; this resulted in students who were more focused and less frustrated.

The holiday-themed art projects required the young students to plan and acquire supplies and resulted in paper trees that looked as if they came from an art museum and a leprechaun box on Saint Patrick's Day. They also had the science, music, and gym teachers incorporate similar strategies in the bigger groups, and they were getting impressive results.

I wondered how two teachers and several aides could handle a class with twelve kids, each of whom had a learning disability, split among three grades. Their organization, experience, and passion brought results. At the end of the year, they had a show packed with entertainment with kids covering classroom highlights using popular rock tunes, hilarious skits, sound effects, and impressive stage sets. I started laughing like a hyena and ultimately cried tears of happiness from all the talent on display. Mrs. Collin saw me in tears, and all I could say was I had not cried like that since the chapel at DuPont Hospital. She replied with one sentence: "Shannon's progress is remarkable!"

Shannon joined me for a workout shoveling snow with impressive results

21

CALIFORNIA ADVENTURES

In the fall of 2005, with Shannon now in third grade, the cold weather arrived early, and Shannon's agitation increased with limited outdoor activities to pursue. I decided on a trip to California for a family vacation in November on a scheduled break from school due to teachers' conventions concurrent with Veterans Day and Election Day. We flew across the country on a red-eye, hoping the kids would sleep the entire way. We rented a minivan and checked into a nice hotel in Valencia. Jan had some friends there from her days as a flight attendant, and I had a nephew there we planned on visiting.

The trip was also a celebration of the resolution of the legal case against the driver of the automobile that had struck Shannon. Barry was not able to get much cooperation from the driver's insurance company. He brought in a high-powered attorney from Philadelphia who had all kinds of litigation experience. Over a three-year period, the case became a real commitment with depositions and evaluations Shannon had to undergo for both sides of experts to determine the extent of her injuries, a reconstruction of the traffic accident scene, and discussions of nonbinding arbitration. The case was finally settled just before the trial was scheduled. The settlement, while fair, wiped out my load of medical debt, which was an enormous relief. Attorney's fees or expenses also took a large chunk of the settlement, even though Barry forwent his authorized fees for being the first lawyer on the case. What an amazing brother! There was a mediocre-size balance remaining, which we put away for Shannon's future education expenses.

We stayed at a Hyatt hotel in Valencia close to one of Jan's friends. It had a courtyard that seemed to be out of the movies. It had a large grassy area with several orange trees leading to a brick patio with tables and a pond with a fountain. On the first day, Shannon, Tim, and I hit the courtyard and found some more large orange trees with gigantic oranges hanging as low as six feet. I could not resist picking them and tossing them to the heavens above. I was surprised at the height they ascended to and the velocity with which they returned. Knowing the kids would love to see me catch them, I parked myself under their downward trajectory and braced myself for impact. The oranges hit my outstretched hands or arms and exploded on impact. Shannon and Tim laughed their heads off as the orange juice splattered across the courtyard and the other orange components also burst and spread. Next, we played catch with the smaller oranges, hoping they would remain intact—with mixed results. Tim found the water fountain and dozens of small rocks to throw in it. He suggested including the oranges too for a bigger splash. I redirected them to a mini obstacle course I had created with the smashed oranges marking turn points and the patio tables and chairs involved. We had races from one end of the course to the next with Shannon winning each time.

After twenty minutes the oranges were even more dispersed and lots of napkins and plastic cutlery were on the patio ground. Just as we were wrapping up, a hotel manager walked out and said into his direct-connect Nextel phone, "Send a maintenance team out to the courtyard. It is a mess with crushed oranges and napkins everywhere."

What a great excursion on our first day. I had a real feeling of happiness as Shannon was in her glory enjoying improvised activities and Tim was enjoying recreation that he would not have experienced if Shannon had never been injured. I had a nephew working an internship in nearby Los Angeles. He visited us, arriving just as we headed to the pool, laughing about the orange tree adventure. I had to rinse the orange juice off. He had not seen Shannon for some time due to his being away at college and was impressed with her confidence in the pool. We had the pool to ourselves as a few guests sat in the chairs, ordered cocktails, and complained about our noisy splashing.

We went to Anaheim a few days later and visited the Disney parks. There was no crowd, so the kids got constant close-ups with the characters. Tim, two at the time, surprised us with his participation and jumped right in. Shannon did get tired and needed her rest. Tim had to continue his character search-and-find mission with just his dad. Later that night we returned to the park with a refreshed Shannon for the electric light parade, which was awesome. Shannon and Tim had their first exposure to room service and soon were making frequent calls with detailed instructions on what they wanted. They would clap with great enthusiasm when the room service attendant arrived. I was spending money at a rapid pace, which concerned me, but the added stimulation was what Shannon needed.

She returned to New Jersey with tales for her teachers and classmates of Disney characters, smashed oranges, and room service variety. All of this was continuous stimulation for her brain that she could not have gotten in the cold Northeast. We got a sign the plan was working one night as we relaxed in the hotel room and Shannon read a book out loud herself. It was called *I Should Be in the Zoo*. It was a book I read to her repeatedly so she could memorize the words. I still celebrated like she had just earned her PhD. Shannon replied, "Dad, calm down."

After a successful third-grade year, Shannon attended a summer program and did fine with reinforcement of reading, math, and English concepts. She planned a trip to Hershey Park, Pennsylvania, and stuck with the water park activities as her mom and brother went on the smaller, dry rides. That left me to enjoy the rapid slides and descents from challenging heights. Shannon did not shy away from anything, and instead we went down slides together. The car sickness was a thing of the past, and Shannon had a healthy vestibular system controlling her balance from the inner ear, so she was able to enjoy the packed water park.

The hotel we stayed in had a fine reputation, but nothing went right as they assigned us a room that was already occupied by a sleeping older man, closed the indoor pool during an outside rainstorm, and had restaurants that ran out of food and machines that ran out of snacks and a pizza service that did not deliver in the rain. Shannon called it a "wretched" hotel, a word she had learned from her latest Disney movie, *101 Dalmatians*. She planned on telling her classmates and teachers about Hershey Park and the "Wretched Hotel." We took several day trips to Ocean City and watched Shannon take charge as she showed her brother the beach and ocean activities and took him on boardwalk rides with us waving as they circled. Tim was a great addition to the family and a lucky brother to be getting guidance from his sister.

*Shannon outrunning her brother and dad at the hotel courtyard after the
hilarious session of playing catch with gigantic oranges*

22

REPRESENTING THE RONALD

MCDONALD HOUSE IN STYLE

I stayed active with Ronald McDonald House of Delaware by making speeches every few months. Shannon's visits were rare, mainly after her medical checkups every six months or during a special event like their annual Share a Night holiday celebration. She was well known to the house staff and executive board for her inspiring story and enthusiastic greetings. They selected her to greet Duchess Fergie of England when she visited the Philadelphia Ronald McDonald House. Shannon delivered flowers to Fergie's limousine and escorted her inside, where she spoke to the children staying there that week. A few professional clowns were also on hand and took all the kids to the indoor playground for an impromptu magic show followed by a hilarious stair-climbing exercise.

We joined the Philadelphia house on a trip to the circus at the Philadelphia Spectrum over the summer. Outside we got to talk with one of the house founders, who was so happy to meet Shannon, as he was aware of her progress. I commended him on founding such an amazing organization, as it had held our family together and enabled us to help Shannon make such remarkable progress. They deflected credit to the managers and staff members of the individual houses.

We had attended the annual Phillies games on Ronald Mcdonald House Charity night. The ticket included a hot dog, soda, and donation to the house. I had sold up to thirty tickets the last several years. Family and coworkers attended the game at the new Citizens Bank Park. It was a great chance for Shannon to catch up with her aunts and cousins.

Toward the end of Shannon's fifth-grade year in 2007, the Delaware house staff asked if she wanted to throw out the first pitch at that year's game. We said yes with no hesitation whatsoever. I practiced with Shannon every day for over two weeks. She could make the sixty-foot throw as long as she wound up her arm and used her core to make the throw. I sold sixty tickets to mainly the same family and friends who had visited us in the Cooper PICU.

On the day of the event, Shannon proudly wore a red T-shirt with her school's logo, got Jan to prepare her long black hair, and looked ready to share her success with the world. We got to the park on time and found our Phillies organization contact through the house director, Karen. They escorted us to field-level corridors. Standing on the infield was remarkable amid the perfectly manicured grass, surrounded by brightly colored seats on all sides, seeing the athletes preparing for the game, as well as cameramen and announcers preparing equipment. We were surprised to see other people with the same mission. An adult male local radio disc jockey and a young boy around twelve years old also were throwing out pitches on behalf of other organizations.

They proceeded to Shannon. A team official said the pitches had to be made from just before the pitcher's mound, or about fifty-two feet from home plate. The Philly Phanatic was there and seemed to recognize us from prior Ronald McDonald House events. He accosted the adults and shook his enormous stomach for the kids. Four-year-old Tim was with us and watching all. He seemed most fixed on Phillies slugger Ryan Howard, who was stretching in the shallow outfield between first and second base. I asked the escort to let Shannon throw off the mound. She said there was no time for the grounds crew to reprepare the mound. We had practiced at a distance of sixty feet, so I wondered about Shannon's accuracy from ten feet closer. She was talking to Ronald McDonald, who knew us well from prior events.

All of a sudden, Shannon's name appeared on the scoreboard as she walked out to the premound area with Ronald. The same public address announcer who introduced the players announced her name: "*Please welcome Shannon Mulhern, who is throwing out the ceremonial first pitch on behalf of the Ronald McDonald House.*"

Ronald stepped back as Shannon wound up and fired a powerful pitch. I saw her name in very high-tech graphics on the scoreboard and the real-time video of her on the jumbo screens and started to tear up. Her feet were straight without orthopedic braces. She was calm and confident in front of nearly thirty thousand people. She accepted the spotlight and proudly represented the Ronald McDonald House. The Philly Phanatic was acting as the catcher. Shannon's pitch sailed over his head and plunked a cameraman ten feet behind him. The Phanatic started laughing very hard at the cameraman as he approached Shannon with lots of congratulations. Shannon smiled as Ronald and the Phanatic stood at her side for a picture taken by the same cameraman. I thought of how far she had come to have the strength to fire a pitch so high, with more velocity than many people who had thrown off the mound. We heard the cheers from the crowd even though our sixty family members and friends were seated in a section in the upper deck. We stood by as the national anthem was sung by a young lady with a powerful voice.

The escort whisked us off the field to the locker room. Within minutes we arrived at our section near the top of the stadium. I let Shannon run free to visit all and accept congratulations. I had fronted the money for the tickets, so people were paying me back. Soon I had nearly a grand in my pocket. I paid for several rounds of drinks and refreshments so all could celebrate the great night. All of these people had been with us at our lowest point in intensive care, wondering if Shannon would survive. Now they were with us at our highest point as a healthy Shannon represented the Ronald McDonald House at such a high-profile event. We felt as though we had come full circle and were nearing the end of the journey by celebrating on this magnificent night. Shannon was doing fine in school and closing the cognitive and motor skill gap with her peers. She had overcome severe injuries and was serving as a great inspiration to all. The many forms of stimulation we had used had paid off. We hope that other families can find similar progress when the odds are stacked against them. Perseverance, commitment, and Shannon's work ethic did what so many considered impossible. Shannon's future is bright. She is eager to help others overcome the odds and celebrate success!

Shannon is all smiles at the big event.
Photo used with Philadelphia Phillies / MLB permission.

EPILOGUE

Shannon and I watched the CNN anchors and politicians argue about models that predicted over a hundred thousand deaths due to coronavirus. She was entering the homestretch of her requirements for an associate's degree in exercise science and glad spring was here with its outdoor activities. She already had a personal training certification and a part-time job at a local gym showing members how to use circuit machines. Needing a break from her courses, which had been converted to an online format, she turned to the TV and the *Law and Order* series. After a few days' reruns, she turned to me for other options.

"Dad, I see they canceled the telethon for the Ronald McDonald House this year. Why?"

"No crowds of more than ten people are authorized. You have been the center of attention for several telethons now. They are moving on to younger kids." I gave an accurate and disappointing reply.

"I hope it clears up by my graduation ceremony."

I could tell by her facial expressions that Shannon was disappointed about the virus's impact of shutting down all forms of celebration. I hoped that bringing up highlights of her previous high-profile activities could boost her spirits. "You even got to throw out the first pitch for the Phillies on behalf of the Ronald McDonald House."

"Will the coronavirus delay the start of baseball season?"

"Definitely."

"I may go to the mall for some shopping."

"The mall is closed too."

"At least I can go to the gym and work out."

"The gym is closing too."

"Dad, that is everything I do. No attending class at school, no gym, no mall—we can't even watch baseball. What are we going to do?"

"We are going to find a silver lining, like we always do. Tomorrow we will go to Walmart, which is still open, and buy all the equipment you need for a personal gym at home. You can practice driving on the streets, as they are empty, and it will build your driving confidence. Remember our last sort-of-quarantine the whole summer from July Fourth to Labor Day in the hospital? You shocked all the doctors, therapists, and nurses with your recovery skills. This period can be productive."

"OK, Dad, but we can't even watch the Phillies."

"You are right, but we will find activity."

"The only thing on TV seems to be Trump and the reporters arguing about whether China is responsible and whose fault it is that there is not enough PPE."

"You're right again, Shan; time to read some books."

"Are the library and bookstore open?"

"No, both closed; don't you have any new books?"

"No, I read them all. Guess I can listen to music or do some artwork or check Facebook and Instagram."

"Yes, those options are still valid and not touched by the coronavirus."

"How did you and Mom get through my hospitalization, Dad? What did you and Mom do?"

"Good question, Shan…"

UPDATE:

BACK TO COOPER, MARCH 2021

Just as I thought that medical challenges were behind me, Tim called me at 10:30 p.m. sounding stressed out to advise me he was in a car with five buddies en route to Philadelphia when the driver accelerated, lost control, flipped the car, and crashed into a guardrail. The ambulance was taking him to Cooper Trauma Center. He thought his wrist was broken. I told him to stay calm as I raced to my car and sped off to join him. He called me and sounded clear headed, coherent, and calm, so he was fine neurologically. I recalled the last time I had gotten such a call and sped off to the same destination. That was a life-changing moment. The traffic was light as I wondered who had been driving, why they were going to Philly without my approval, and what injuries my eighteen-year-old might be suffering from. How would I tell Jan and Shannon about this?

I found the hospital exit and saw unrecognizable parts of the hospital. It had undergone a gigantic modernization. I followed the ER signs and considered parking in the ambulance bay but continued to the public entrance and immediately found a spot. I bolted to the ER entrance, which was just a foyer, with the actual ER sealed off. A security guard behind a partition asked if I needed assistance. I told her I had to join my son, who had been transported via ambulance after a motor vehicle accident. She took my cell phone number and said, "A nurse will call you. Only patients are allowed in the ER due to coronavirus restrictions."

I went back to the lot and started pacing the same ground I had paced all night twenty years ago, praying for Shannon's survival. I wondered whether the plaque we gave to the PICU staff many years ago in recognition of Shannon's recovery was still prominently displayed, providing inspiration to parents. Could anyone from that long ago still be here and remember me to facilitate ER access? Family members of other patients were also on parking lot patrol, talking on their cell phones and expressing frustration they had been denied access.

I felt the tension in my arms and legs but did not have the extreme nausea and chills up my spine that Shannon's accident had made my constant companion for weeks. I knew that Tim was not seriously injured, as he had called me and sounded clear, and no medical personnel had come running out to get permission for invasive procedures. My cell phone rang.

"Mr. Mulhern, your son appears to have a fractured wrist, as well as back soreness. We will take some x-rays and place a cast on his wrist and most likely discharge him in a few hours."

All I could reply was "Thank you." Time to notify Jan and Shannon and hope they stayed calm.

"Shannon, it's me."

"Dad, where did you run out to? I heard you leave so fast. Is it Grandpa?"

"Grandpa is fine. Tim was in a car accident and broke his wrist. Mom won't answer her phone."

"She went to sleep. Should I wake her?" Shannon sounded clear headed and focused.

"No, we better let her get her rest."

"OK, Dad. Just take care of Tim at the hospital. Is he staying overnight?"

"No, we should be back in a few hours."

"That's good. What hospital?"

"Cooper Trauma Center."

"Wow, that's where I went in a helicopter and spent a week in a coma. Thank God Tim is not seriously hurt. Are you OK, Dad? You must be having some memories."

"They're good memories, Shannon—you made the whole journey one of hard work, results, and togetherness. You set a great example for all."

ACKNOWLEDGMENTS

Many planned projects become difficult to complete when career and parental responsibilities demand attention. The list of people who deserve my gratitude is long, starting most recently and working backward with the faculty at the Rowan Master of Arts Writing Program, which helped me shake off thirty-five years of rust as a college student and channel my enthusiasm for the writing arts to a master's degree, an adjunct professor position, and a completed manuscript. My much-younger peers were so supportive with helpful suggestions, especially Taylor Henry and Kayla Harrison. Never forget meeting your description standards after 170 pages. All my professors were on target, with Deb Martin, Heather Lanier, Megan Atwood, Drew Kopp, Ron Block, Steve Royek, Amy Woodworth, and Jen Courtney taking me beyond my program goals.

My colleagues at US Customs shared my vision and encouraged the pursuit of this book project. No better way to deal with current job stressors than off-the-job endeavors. Thanks for the daily conversations I have grown to miss from airport to seaport to the range to the Customs house. Thanks especially to Jack Gallagher, John Hughes, John Fenningham (RIP), and Tony Tangi for joining me on the midnight ride at Cooper during Shannon's first week of hospitalization. Megan DiPatri, your many visits at both hospitals provided a boost we needed.

Team Shannon was vast and awesome. Therapists, teachers, trainers, and coaches all provided fun therapy sessions starting in the hospital and transitioning to dance class, softball, and cheerleading. Matt Wright and Linda Cregar, there was no drop in intensity or results when we moved from physical therapy to personal training. Mr. Schuenemann and Mrs. Saville, you were so supportive of Shannon at high school. We think of you often as you still help us from heaven. Coach Ed Obermann is with you, and he taught Shannon to drill a softball off a tee or pitch.

Judy, your group and private dance lessons were just what Shannon needed. Theresa, your cheerleading team built her confidence. Many teachers went the extra mile, especially Mrs. Linda Cullen, Mrs. Eileen Collarin, Mrs. Finn, Mrs. Dotto, Mr. Volpe, Mr. Ippolite, Mrs. Tavaras, Mrs. Holmes, Mr. Barnes, Mrs. Consiglio, and Mrs. Mulvihill. Thanks for your consistent support.

Staff and volunteers at the Ronald McDonald House of Delaware, thanks for your committed efforts. We benefited from all facets of the house, from the art on the walls to the flowers on the tables to the playroom to the great meals to the emotional support to Kirby the magnificent therapy dog and Mary his handler with the heart of gold to the many events we attended with Shannon proudly representing the house on TV and social media and at the Phillies game. Trish McEvers, you were an angel who lifted us at our darkest moments. Thanks for that power and for encouraging me to be a Delaware House spokesperson.

The staff at DuPont Hospital was an amazing group of professionals that worked together to overcome grim prognoses. All the nurses and therapists were answers to our prayers. Nurses Cathy and Jill, PT Elizabeth, Mary, and OT Suzy all found ways to work through the darkness to the light. Doctors at DuPont guided all to stay committed and surpass goals. Dr. Alexander, thanks for running an amazing rehab unit. Thanks to Dr. McManus for maintaining it.

The staff at Cooper Trauma Center cared for Shannon at most-critical moments and prepped us for the battles ahead. Nurse Sue and Dr. Mirza, not a day goes by when I don't think of you with gratitude.

Barry, thanks for the daily visits, starting with two a day at Cooper, and your professional expertise, which made the admin nightmare just another challenge we could overcome. You added to the team John DiDonato, who resolved the complex case and mountain of medical bills. Thanks, John.

Anne, thanks for your in-depth medical knowledge and early efforts to keep Shannon's feet straight and the push to move to DuPont. You clearly were the most knowledgeable therapist out of the dozens we eventually worked with.

Mary Ellen, Patty, Betty, Marge, Frank, Joan, and Kate, thanks for always responding to the call, whether it was for pillows or socks, snacks, or prayers we needed. You always delivered. Thanks to my mom and dad, who raised such an amazing family of professionals that surpass their proficiency with generosity. Thanks to Jan's parents for giving her the strength to reach out to so many struggling parents in their worst moments. Tara, thanks for the nightly vigil and months of care that helped Shannon respond and wake up to lots of love. Thanks, Mazen, Majid, Abraham, Rema, and Lana, for the prayers from overseas and helpful visits. Cousins Satanay and Sasha, your stays with us were welcome, productive, and successful. Thanks for the hours of play activity.

Our son, Tim, has adopted the work ethic of Team Shannon to help her, and positive results have spilled into all facets of his endeavors. Jan stayed strong in the blizzard of stress and took care of our family. Thanks to Shannon, who has shown resilience, drive, heart, and personality in recovering and inspiring all.

Shannon, Tim, Jan, and Paul celebrating
Shan's community college and Tim's high school graduation

RESOURCES

Amen, Daniel. 2010. *Change Your Brain, Change Your Body*. New York: Three Rivers Press.

———. 2013. *Unleash the Power of the Female Brain*. New York: Harmony Books.

Doman, Glenn. 2005. *What to Do about Your Brain Injured Child*. New Garden City Park, NY: Square One Publishers.

Goldstein, Joel. 2012. *No Stone Unturned: A Father's Memoir of His Son's Encounter with a Traumatic Brain Injury*. Dullus, VA: Potomac Books.

Guilmette, Thomas. 1997. *Pocket Guide to Brain Injury: Cognitive and Neurological Rehabilitation*. San Diego, CA Singular Publishing Group.

Lind-Kyle, Patt. 2009. *Heal Your Mind, Rewire Your Brain*. Santa Rosa, CA: Energy Psychology Press.

Medina, John. 2009. *Brain Rules*. Seattle, WA: Pear Press.

Mason, Michael Paul. 2008. *Head Cases: Stories of Brain Injury and Its Aftermath*. New York: Farrar, Straus and Giroux.

Murray, Jimmy, and Steve McWilliams. 2019. *Life Is an Audible.* Newtown Square, PA: Harrowwood Books.

Ratey, John. 2002. *A User's Guide to the Brain.* New York: Vintage Books.

———. 2008. *Spark: The Revolutionary New Science of Exercise and the Brain.* Little, New York: Brown & Co.

Strauch, Barbara. 2010. *The Secret Life of the Grown-Up Brain.* New York: Penguin Books.

Sweeney, Michael. 2009. *Brain: The Complete Mind.* Washington, DC: National Geographic Society.

Made in the USA
Columbia, SC
07 October 2024

43226948R00122